DECARBONOMICS

DECARBONOMICS

& THE POST-PANDEMIC WORLD

Charles Dumas

P
PROFILE BOOKS

First published in Great Britain in 2021 by
Profile Books Ltd
29 Cloth Fair
London EC1A 7JQ
www.profilebooks.com

Copyright © TSL Research Group Limited, 2021

The moral right of the author has been asserted.

All rights reserved. Without limiting the rights under copyright reserved above, no part of this publication may be reproduced, stored or introduced into a retrieval system, or transmitted, in any form or by any means (electronic, mechanical, photocopying, recording or otherwise), without the prior written permission of both the copyright owner and the publisher of this book.

Typeset in Garamond by MacGuru Ltd
Printed and bound in Britain by
CPI Group (UK) Ltd, Croydon, CR0 4YY

A CIP catalogue record for this book is available from the British Library.

ISBN 978 1 80081 059 4
eISBN 978 1 80081 060 0

Contents

Introduction: From sacrifice to opportunity	1
Essay 1: The post-pandemic world	12
Essay 2: Climate change	66
Appendix 1: Bill Gates' 'to do' list	109
Appendix 2: Carbon taxes and inequality	126
Index	130

Introduction: From sacrifice to opportunity

The cost of electricity generated by solar panels and (onshore) wind turbines fell below its cost using coal and natural gas in 2018–19. This shift, with similar, tech-driven cuts in battery costs, transforms climate-change economics from a story of necessary sacrifice at least partly to one of opportunity. As Figure 2 (overleaf) shows for projected renewables-electricity costs, improved technology should reduce a host of 'green' costs as a result of the combat with climate change over forthcoming decades.

In this book, Essay 1 covers the post-pandemic economy, and Essay 2 the economics of climate change. The linkage between the two parts is not just that they are both important and follow on from one another. It has become clear that despite the boost to potential growth arising from the benefits of tech-sector progress, advanced economies have become anaemic, with budget deficits apparently indispensable to ensuring adequate demand. Prosperity throughout the twentieth century depended not just on supply-side progress and productivity growth; it also arose

Figure 1 **Electricity costs per megawatt-hour**
Various energy sources (averaged)

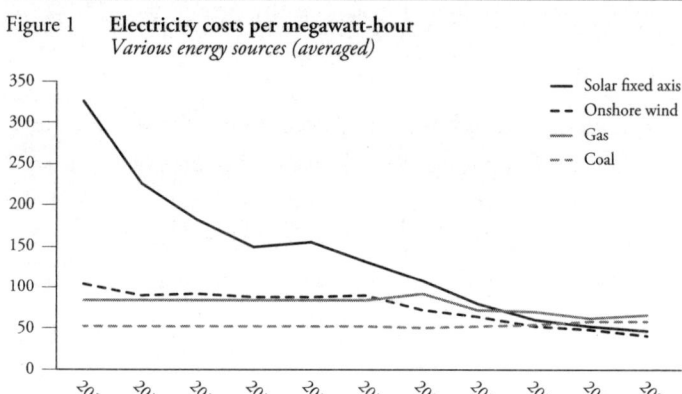

Sources: Carbon Tracker, Bloomberg, TS Lombard

Figure 2 **High and low prospective solar and coal costs of electricity**
$/MWh

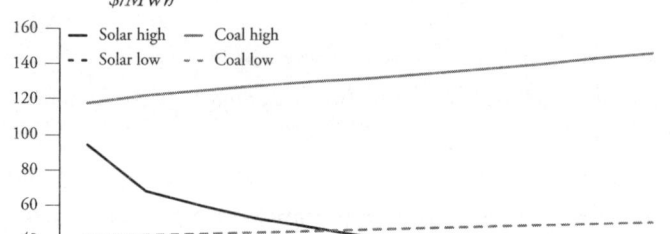

Sources: Carbon Tracker, TS Lombard

from the world being transformed by the destruction of assets in two world wars, and by the rebalancing of political power that ensued.

Commentators and analysts in the first half of the nineteenth century, including Karl Marx in his productive early years, worried that in a capitalist economy demand might fall short of fully utilising potential supply. Their intuition was sound. In 1928 Frank Ramsey, a Cambridge colleague of Keynes (and philosophy supervisor of Wittgenstein) produced a now-famous algebraic analysis of savings that said broadly (without the algebra) that we save too little. He died two years later aged only twenty-six.

It often puzzles non-economists that saving is identical with investment – crucially, this is necessarily true, but only after the event (*ex post*), no matter what we might have wished for *ex ante*. (Auberon Waugh, eldest son of Evelyn Waugh, gave up on the economics part of his Oxford University PPE course – Politics, Philosophy and Economics – precisely because he could not understand this identity.) Arguably, people have an intuitive sense of Ramsey's analysis and are vaguely (or precisely) conscious of the need to save more. But what if many of the best tech capital spending (capex) opportunities lie not so much in new products requiring capex but in making better use of existing capital assets, e.g. Uber and Lyft for drivers already owning cars, or Airbnb for people with spare rooms or just wanting to finance a holiday abroad by letting out their home? The return on existing capital could remain high in this scenario, while the desire to save simply turns out to mean a shortage of demand. That investment is identical to saving in aggregate would show

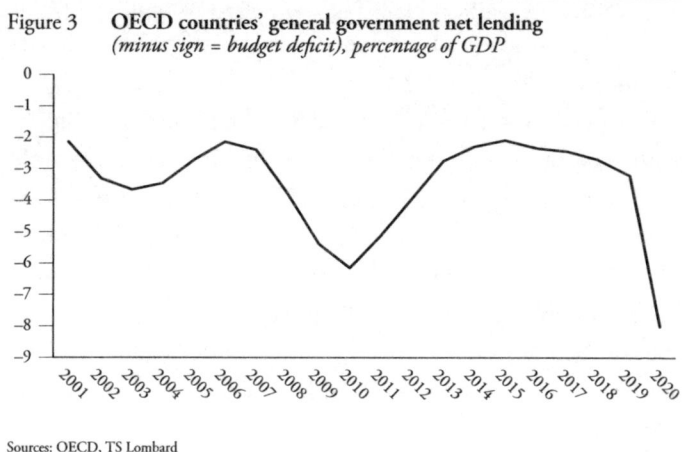

Figure 3   OECD countries' general government net lending *(minus sign = budget deficit), percentage of GDP*

Sources: OECD, TS Lombard

up as an unwanted build-up of unsold inventory: stockbuilding that would be an unwelcome and unproductive form of capex. Nominal and real interest rates could become negligible, as demand weakens and the return on new capex weakens with it. If this sounds familiar, that is because it is.

One result of these tendencies is that advanced economies are now chronically dependent on budget deficits to sustain demand and full employment, despite rejection since the 2007–09 global financial crisis (GFC) of Keynesian remedies to disinflation and/or deflation. Figures 3 (above) and 4 (opposite) show how this has led to progressively higher debt levels, both in the non-financial private sector and especially governments. In Essay 1 we will see how for advanced economies the sluggish ten-to-twelve-year recovery from the GFC has to a great

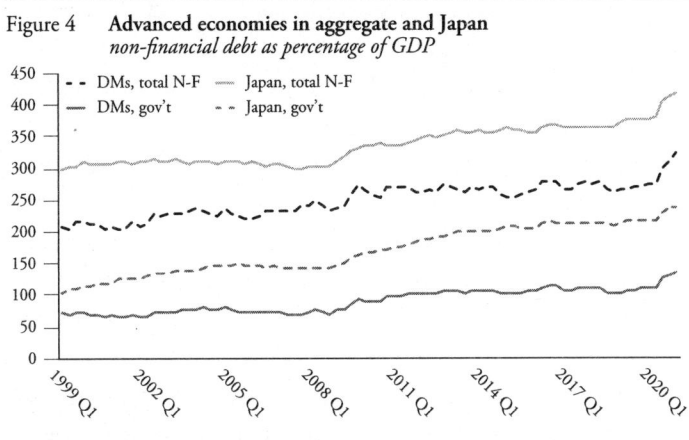

Figure 4 **Advanced economies in aggregate and Japan**
non-financial debt as percentage of GDP

Sources: BIS, TS Lombard

extent been caused by too-strict fiscal policies. Yet dependence on budget deficits persists and has been aggravated by Covid-19. Without a new source of investment demand, this could become an acute policy quandary. Even with the significant boost to capex that we expect from replacement of fossil-fuelled electricity generation, large debts could put countries in difficulties should more lively capex cause interest rates to rebound to more normal levels, as is likely.

Cue a fresh wave of 'creative destruction' in Schumpeter's resonant phrase. With the descent of renewables-generated electricity costs below that of fossil fuels – a disparity expected to grow rapidly in the 2020s – the entire existing energy infrastructure of the world becomes potentially obsolete – 'stranded assets' in the current jargon. The clear political commitment to net-zero carbon emissions by mid-century in most advanced countries (and by 2060 in China's case) requires that these stranded assets are replaced. It is entirely possible that extreme weather events beyond the scale of those anticipated by the meteorological scientists that forecast global warming will create earlier pressure for action.

The scale of commitment will be analysed in Essay 2, but 2020 was a watershed, after which climate-change denialists will be permanently on the defensive in an anti-science cul-de-sac: the Covid-19 crisis has discredited people that wilfully ignore scientific evidence. Nonetheless, the plausibility of the various routes proposed to achieve net zero will be an important part of the analysis, as will be the arguments over the timing of this goal. But the emergence of renewable-sourced electricity as cheaper than fossil fuels ensures that the replacement of obsolescent capacities will happen anyhow simply to minimise costs. What political resistance to such changes may achieve could prove to be a mere timing issue.

An important consideration in relation to the economics of climate change is the size of the world's population, currently 7.8 billion people and forecast to be 11 billion by the end of the century. Stern's seminal report on climate change of late 2006 gave little analysis of how climate change, or increased global affluence generally, might affect population growth. And World Bank data on carbon emissions are frequently cited on a per capita basis, as this permits comparisons (often invidious) between different countries' policies and performance. But population growth is self-evidently a major factor in global warming, once man-made carbon emissions are held responsible (as by most relevant scientists). Ever since the theories of Thomas Malthus became popular in the early nineteenth century, population growth, its causes and effects, have been central to economics – and this remains true (Essay 2).

Specifically (Essay 2) one of the chief sources of greenhouse gas (GHG) emissions is now the manufacturing of cement (about 8 per cent of worldwide CO_2 emissions) and steel (about 10 per cent). Agriculture's 19 per cent of GHGs (much of it methane and nitrous oxide, each a much more potent GHG than CO_2) is also strongly affected by population growth. As much of the cement and steel is for construction, very much depending on population growth, this is a major issue in climate-change analysis. A long-term reduction of population growth, let alone an actual cut in the world's population, would clearly ease climate change.

An important part of the context of the debate on how to combat climate change is the age-old question of who's to blame. Alarm about climate change, while scientifically valid, has hitherto largely been spread by people that could (ungenerously) be described as quasi-religious about the environment. A complication is that less-developed countries (LDCs) can quite reasonably say that advanced economies are responsible for the carbon emissions that have caused climate change, yet at the same time they want to achieve advanced-country income levels. As a result resistance to generalised measures to combat climate change has arisen from a combination of climate change denialists – hoping that with 'benign neglect' the problem will go away – and LDCs whose priority is catch-up growth. If the scientists are right about the long-run effects of climate change, then LDCs will suffer the most, but some of these effects would emerge only after hundreds, or even thousands, of years, so the temptation is very strong to back-burner the issue – to make hay while the sun shines. On a more positive note, China's new awareness of the threat of climate change is mirrored by similar changes of political mood in Brazil, Russia and Indonesia, favouring action sooner rather than later.

The International Energy Agency (IEA) has recently published an analysis of what it calls a 'narrow path' leading to 'net-zero' GHG emissions by 2050, the target that could limit overall global warming to 1½°C from the widely accepted mid-nineteenth-century baseline. (Warming to 2020 has been 1.1–1.2° and is accelerating.) The consequences of greater global warming than 1½° are described at the end of Essay 2. This target is widely accepted as being what is necessary to combat climate change. Yet many people are completely unaware of what is implied by global warming depending on the *stock* of GHGs in the atmosphere, as opposed to the *flow* of fresh GHGs. Reducing GHG flows to 'net zero' is simply what is needed to stop increasing the stock of GHGs in the atmosphere. Much of the long-run damage from climate change will occur if the concentration of atmospheric GHGs stays at the level likely should that 'net zero' target be achieved – even the IPCC's projected optimal policy mix would see the world temperature rising until 2075. (A particular threat would be a 'tipping point' of ice on land melting in Greenland or the Antarctic, causing a major rise in the world's sea level – whereas the melting of Arctic ice has had little effect on the world's sea level as Arctic ice floats on water, being less dense – hence the fact that it floats!)

To prevent this long-run damage, the world will need to move on from 'net zero' immediately to 'net negative' GHG emissions. People seem to think that getting to net zero means 'job done' – when that will (if the science is right) simply mark the 'end of the beginning'!

While climate change poses huge challenges that will profoundly affect the world and its economies for centuries, recent economic policies have been far from a failure by conventional standards. What have we had for the forty years since Thatcher/Reagan in 1979–80? Depending on whether you're on the left or the right, it has been either neo-liberal policies or free-market monetarism – in both cases combined with globalisation, until the Sino–US trade war started in 2018.

Whatever your political stance, what might have been expected? And what actually happened? Clearly, one would expect lots of jobs in low-wage countries and huge asset-price gains for those owning productive capital assets suddenly in short supply vis-à-vis the four-times multiple of available labour (from countries with 1 billion of population to 4 billion-plus) with the inclusion of China, many Asean countries, the old Comintern, and lastly India into the functioning, globalised world economy.

And so it has proved – showing the essential idealism of utilitarian economists of a Friedmanite stripe. Inequality has increased in every major country, but a hugely increased share of income in poorer countries (emerging markets – EMs in Figure 5, overleaf) means inequality has probably been reduced globally. (Global inequality is not measured by the World Bank.) And absolute poverty now afflicts less than 10 per cent of the

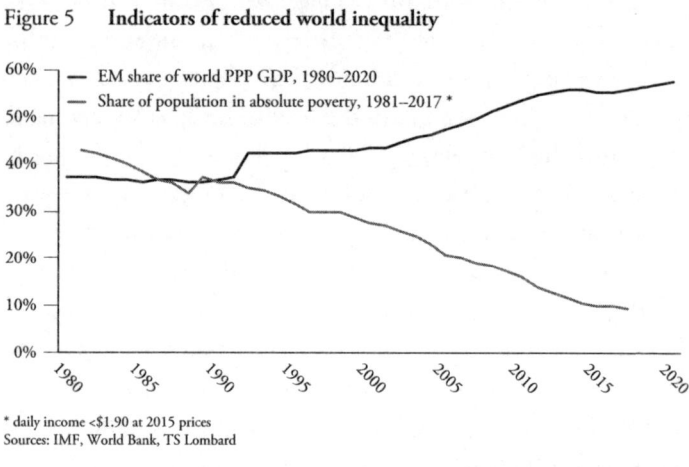

Figure 5 Indicators of reduced world inequality

— EM share of world PPP GDP, 1980–2020
— Share of population in absolute poverty, 1981–2017 *

* daily income <$1.90 at 2015 prices
Sources: IMF, World Bank, TS Lombard

world's people, versus more than 40 per cent in the early 1980s. This downtrend may have been interrupted by the Covid-19 recession, but should soon resume. In the 1980s, it was the agricultural 'green revolution' that cut poverty, preceding the benefits of post-1990 globalisation.

Radical tech innovations in parallel with globalisation reinforced the anti-Keynesian bias of monetarist/supply-side policy bequeathed by the great inflation of the 1960s and 70s. But both globalisation and tech contributed to the relative stagnation of mid-wage, advanced-country incomes. So in the democracies of the West the trends just described led to populist reactions, which threaten to unwind some of the benefits of free-market liberalism (neo or otherwise) and in the US case are a major cause of the Sino–US trade war. This is the essential background to the current convulsions in economic policy, as well as the analysis in my 2018 book, *Populism and Economics*. The success story of the past thirty to forty years is the rapid growth of LDCs and reduction of poverty. But policies in advanced economies have been less successful, though the lip service to combat climate change has helped create, via public subsidies, the success story of cheap, renewables-based electricity.

Essay 1

The post-pandemic world

The 2020 recessions arising from the Covid-19 pandemic (and the policy response to it) have been the most serious for several hundred years – at least as regards economies for which estimates go back that far. In the advanced countries the bulk of the decline was concentrated in April 2020, though in China it was largely contained in the first quarter (Q1). Before any discussion of the crisis, it is necessary to understand the context. Advanced countries had a seriously disappointing recovery from 2007–09's GFC. For many economies, e.g. Germany and so-called 'commodity countries' (such as Australia), that recovery was spurred by China's strong fiscal response to the GFC in 2008–09. Major flaws in that response emerged in 2015–16. These were thus important in 2009–19's continued weak world recovery just before Covid-19's emergence, which of course was in Wuhan, capital of Hubei province in China, which neighbours Nanjing, the country's 'southern capital'.

The weakness of advanced-country growth after 2011 owed much to aggressive tightening of budgets from 2011 onwards, and also to the peaking that year of China's growth rate, and with it the oil-price and industrial-commodity 'super-cycle'. This was followed by the near seize-up of China's finances in 2015 and early 2016. The imbalances that caused the GFC never came close to being addressed – i.e. the excess saving relative to investment needs that had built up in Japan, German-centred Europe (roughly Germany times two, as it includes Benelux, Scandinavia, Switzerland and Austria) and the 'Asian Tiger' economies, as well as China itself. These excess savings led, via cheap goods and cheap money to buy them with, to fast-growing household debts in the US and excessive debts in various forms in Europe. The 'savings glut' was thus offset by too much debt until the debt was too blatantly excessive for financial markets to continue denying that it was unjustified. (The crisis was also worsened by a muddle over the right policy response – all laid out in my 2010 book, *Globalisation Fractures*.)

After the crisis, given the large debts of the US, the UK/Ireland and Mediterranean Europe, the desirable recovery process should have involved much greater spending by the savings-glut countries. But among the big three, Japan, Germany and China, when it came to spurring more spending, Japan 'would have but couldn't', while Germany 'could have but wouldn't'. Only China boosted spending massively – and mostly in the wrong way, as explained below. Luckily, the US was strong enough to adopt major budget-deficit boosts to demand, with Obama commanding majorities in both the House of Representatives and the Senate, and this was probably a major factor in the world's avoidance of a depression.

After Republican successes in 2010's mid-term US elections, 2011 saw a Congress v. president confrontation over the debt

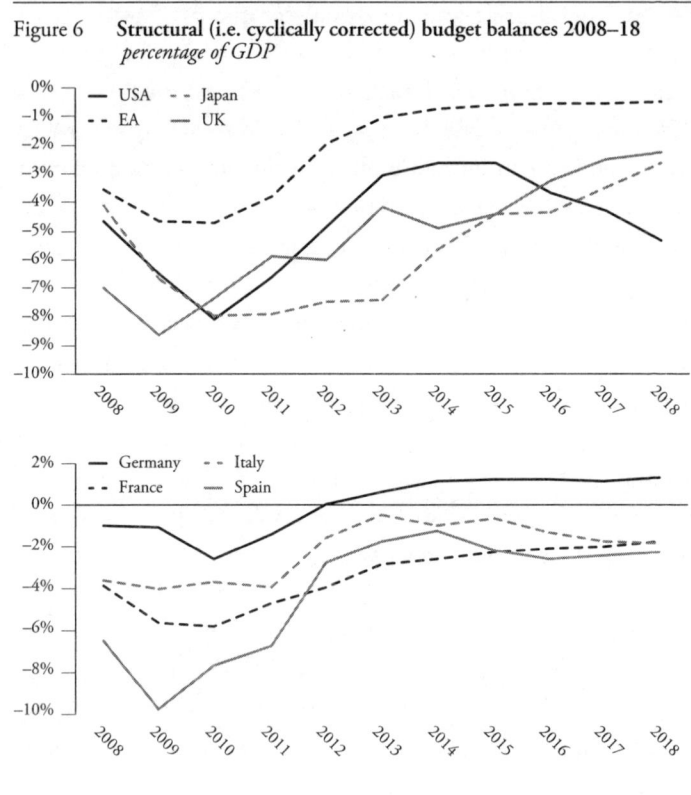

Figure 6 **Structural (i.e. cyclically corrected) budget balances 2008–18**
percentage of GDP

ceiling, Republicans having swept up majorities in both House and Senate, spurred on by the Tea Party claiming to be bent on balanced budgets. Meanwhile, the euro crisis raged in the EA. Germany, having passed a constitutional amendment banning budget deficits in 2009, insisted on its approach being matched by other EA countries in a fiscal compact that precipitated the

EA into double-dip recession for the six quarters, 2011 Q4 to 2013 Q1.

Figure 6 (opposite) shows OECD estimates of the cyclically corrected budget balances in the key period, including 2008–10 when the GFC-induced adoption of budget deficits occurred, as well as the tight budgeting on both sides of the Atlantic from 2011 onwards. The cyclically adjusted balance represents the public-finance policy stance, i.e. the balance between taxation and spending at full employment. It excludes elements of the actual realised deficit that are caused by recession, such as tax revenue shortfalls and relief spending – the so-called automatic stabilisers. The US structural deficit was cut in three years from over 10 per cent of GDP in 2010 to 4 per cent in 2013. Over the same three years, the EA's structural deficit was cut from 5 per cent of GDP to about ½ per cent, with Germany moving into sustained surplus.

In China the post-GFC problem was that the economy was already 'musclebound' on a scale that would have put Charles Atlas to shame: capex rose from an already excessive 40 per cent-plus of GDP to nearly half in 2007. Figure 7 (overleaf) illustrates how the period of above-10 per cent real growth carried on through the GFC, only ending in 2011 Q4, with 9.9 per cent year-on-year real-GDP growth. The post-GFC recovery was based on huge stimulus to gross capital spending, which (including inventory building) rose from about 40 per cent of GDP in 2005–07 to 47 per cent in 2010–11. Imports were sucked in by this. Net exports fell from around 8 per cent of GDP in 2006–08 to an average of 3 per cent of GDP in 2010–11, with 2011 the peak of the energy and metal-price boom, the so-called commodity supercycle.

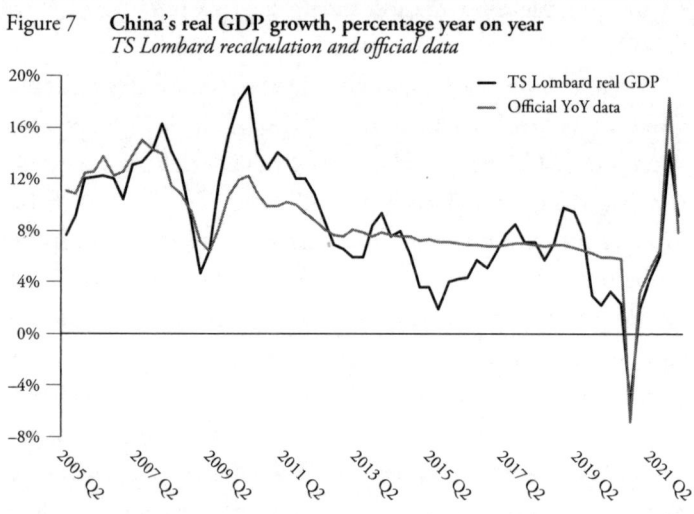

Figure 7 **China's real GDP growth, percentage year on year**
TS Lombard recalculation and official data

There was a flavour of digging holes in the ground and filling them in again about this post-GFC Chinese recovery. But the stimulus to the rest of the world – industrial Europe and Asia as well as energy and commodity countries – was welcome enough, so not too many tough questions were asked. But China's previously highly profitable exports fell from over a third of GDP in the run-up to the GFC to less than a quarter of it by 2013–14, partly reflecting a large upswing of China's real FX rate. Meanwhile in mid-decade, capex ratios stayed around 45 per cent of GDP, and could not conceivably be yielding profitable assets, despite cheap credit.

Total non-financial debt in China, already lifted by the GFC

Figure 8   Total non-financial debt as percentage of Chinese GDP

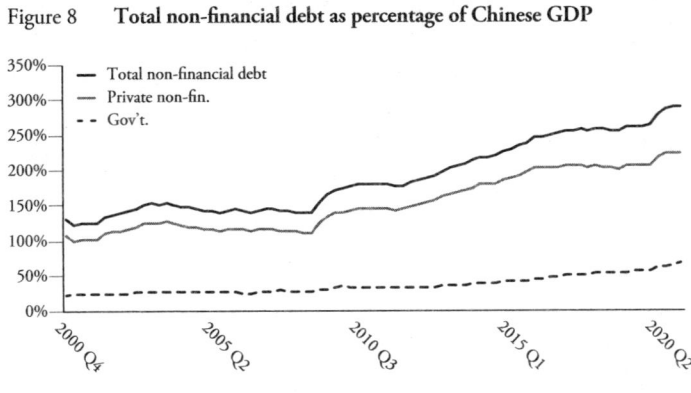

recovery programme from 140 per cent to 185 per cent of GDP in 2010, rose steadily from the end of 2011 to 250 per cent by 2016 (Figure 8). Without this it is unlikely growth momentum could have been maintained. But as Japanese experience had already shown since the mid-1990s, the rising debt level was not a crisis in itself because China had huge net reserves and net foreign assets, reinforced by strong capital controls. Oddly, it was in the stock market – a bit of a sideshow in China – that trouble struck. Unwisely, the authorities had complemented their tolerance of the debt run-up by also talking up the stock market, which had fallen by more than a third in 2010–14.

Between spring 2014 and a year later the Shanghai Composite index rose from a little over 2,000 to just over 5,000. It then relapsed more than 20 per cent by mid-July 2015 (as well it might after such a meteoric boom). The authorities, their hopes thwarted, took what looked like panic measures, and the 'miracle' period was over for China. With the US also slowing from mid-2014 to early 2016 and Europe engaged in aggressive beggar-my-neighbour devaluation (in effect, exporting deflation), 2015's real GDP growth in China fell below 3 per cent. Fortunately for the productive elements of the world economy, this combination of weaknesses, partly reflecting the US–European fiscal tightening described above, caused a crash in energy and metal prices that substantially enhanced real consumer incomes, also cutting costs in productive parts of the world. With fresh Chinese fiscal stimulus and depreciation of the yuan, the world economy rebounded sharply during 2016 and into 2017.

The election of Trump as (a Republican) US president at the end of 2016 represented the first break with the monetarist orthodoxy that Republican Tea Party supporters had imposed on President Obama, and which Hillary Clinton in her campaigning as the Democratic candidate had seemed likely to continue. This policy paradox – Trump to the left of the Democrats – led to tax cuts proposed by Trump in late 2017, with Republicans rallying behind his campaigning success despite their earlier support for balanced-budget principles vis-à-vis Obama. As Figure 6 on structural budget balances shows (page 14) the US cyclically adjusted deficit rose from 4 per cent of GDP in 2013–17 to 6 per cent of GDP in 2018. (While Keynesian deficit stimulus positioned Trump's policies to the left of Hillary Clinton's, the actual 2017 tax cuts were concentrated on corporate income tax, therefore benefiting the rich much more than the poor, though the effective long-run impact of corporate income taxes is complex and unclear.) Trump, with no economic theory but a purely pragmatic approach to policy – 'What works?' – had broken the monetarist hold on economic policy that went back to the inflation of the 1970s and its cure by Paul Volcker from 1980 onwards (see my 2010 book, *Globalisation Fractures*).

2018: trade war, US v. China

As 2018 developed, there was every chance that the US would prove to have adopted, finally, a policy framework for a return to faster growth, after the slowing trend in the first seventeen years of this century, punctuated by the GFC trauma. One of the weaknesses of the US post-GFC recovery had been relatively restrained business fixed capital spending. From mid-2014 through to 2016, business capex slipped back, and its recovery in 2017 was hesitant. But the Philadelphia Federal Reserve, which conducts a monthly survey of business capex intentions, showed them in spring 2018 (in the aftermath of the late-2017 tax cut) to be more positive than at any time in the forty-five years since the early 1970s, just before the first oil crisis of 1973–75. That 1970–73 period was the end of the great post-World War II boom that had run for a quarter-century from 1948.

But it was not to be. Trump in effect undid the benefits of his adoption of Keynesian stimulus by initiating a trade war with China in May 2018. This had always been one of his chief intentions as president. But it stopped business capex growth in its tracks – with good reason, as it turns out, since the trade war has in effect morphed into a broad and deep struggle between the US and China for primacy in the world economy (and, it seems increasingly likely, in the world's geopolitics): as some people put it, a new cold war.

Fragmentation of globalisation

The natural economic result of the Sino–US trade war is that fragmentation replaces globalisation. The original American moves were spurred by the apparent loss of mid-wage jobs and incomes in manufacturing, widely blamed on competition from cheap Asian labour. (Increasingly, analysts argue that it is adoption of tech applications that is rendering these jobs obsolete – see the relevant parts of my 2018 book, *Populism and Economics*.) Notably, in 2016's Democratic primary elections to select the party's presidential candidate, Bernie Sanders, who was a declared socialist well to the left of the American political mainstream, beat Hillary Clinton in Michigan. His pitch was opposition to free trade, which was blamed for imports holding such a large share of US demand.

Trump then went on to be elected president largely by appealing to protectionist sentiments in Midwestern US states, including Michigan. But while the trade war may have held back US growth from mid-2018, the pursuit of reduced trade imbalances with China has broadened into what is now clearly a bipartisan US intention to thwart China's ambition to become the leading world economic power. This is as much a Biden policy as a Trump policy.

This struggle for economic and political primacy threatened to break the world economy into regional blocs even before the Covid-19 crisis. The American desire to see jobs repatriated to the US was backed up by Trump's largely arbitrary imposition of punitive tariffs. This motivates US firms to avoid investing in cheaper sources of supply in Asia for fear of a sudden new tariff. Meanwhile, Chinese firms that were dominating cheap solar panel sales for electricity generation had already, in 2013, worked out how to retain US markets when faced with sudden tariffs arising from US market-share concerns (under President Obama) by shifting final assembly to regional manufacturing locations with good US access such as Malaysia. So the trade war promoted linkage within the China-centred regional economic bloc, and not just within North America or by downgrading global supply chains. Potentially somewhat left out in the cold in all this are the export-dependent Europeans, as well as the less well-placed EMs: what may be fine for south-east Asia is not so fine for Africa and Latin America, for example, however much they profit from exports to China.

The Covid-19 crisis has reinforced this tendency towards regional economic blocs, as well as fostering outright nationalism. The nationalism has most notably taken the form of restrictions on export of key medical equipment (e.g. personal protection equipment – PPE) and vaccines. Also, because economies were arbitrarily closed down by responses to Covid-19, firms have begun to see security of supply as an argument for reducing dependence on elaborate global supply chains that were sometimes unduly vulnerable to lockdowns arising from repeated waves of the pandemic. This goes well beyond fear of arbitrary tariffs (as under Trump in 2018–19) and cuts into both global trade and regional integration within Europe, though favouring it in east Asia.

The 2020 Covid-19 recession favoured China

Apart from the advantage of strict social controls in curbing the medical risks from Covid-19, China had major advantages over the West in monetary and fiscal policy. As a result, it was able to generate a small gain, 1½ per cent, in real 2020 GDP, compared to the recession of 3½ per cent in the US, and 7¾ per cent in the EA. In its monetary policy, China benefited from owning its major banks. So it was able to obtain their forbearance towards service-sector borrowers stressed by revenue losses by simply lifting up the phone and ordering the banks to lend the interest on their debts (so-called ever-greening loans) both to existing zombie firms and service-sector firms stressed by Covid-19. An additional plus was that this left China's budget-deficit capacity free for a large infrastructure programme that spurred domestic recovery.

In contrast, banks in the West are privately owned – their shareholders could not simply be ordered to make dubious loans to firms with income stressed by consumers' cutbacks in service-sector spending. Banks had to be *induced* to show the forbearance that the People's Bank of China could require by simply giving orders. Mostly therefore, budget-deficit capacity in the West was used (some people said overused) to sustain consumer demand, whether by payments to people (as in the US) or underpinning labour costs (as in Europe). Either way, fiscal stimulus was better described as filling in holes in demand than as a large flow of actual spending, as in China.

The benefits of Covid-19 to China's economy went further than this. In China as in the West, consumers were wary of too much social contact with one another. For the West, this meant many incomes were far from fully spent, and household savings rates soared, alongside big increases of unemployment and inequality of income and wealth. In the absence of being able to eat out much or go to the pub – let alone enjoy sports events, cinemas, theatres, etc. – consumers tended to shop online. Such spending as there was, was on goods. One result was major stimulus to Chinese exports. And Chinese consumers were anxious to avoid catching Covid-19 by using trains and other public transport, so they bought lots of cars, providing substantial stimulus to German-centred industrial Europe.

The effect of all this was a distorted recovery. In China, consumers' service-sector reticence was outweighed domestically by the infrastructure boost, as well as by booming exports. In the West, recovery from the April 2020 recession was much more marked in industry, especially manufacturing, than in services – to the benefit, for example, of German-centred Europe, compared to France, Mediterranean Europe and the UK. With 2021's recovery likely to be dominated by service sectors benefiting from the dissemination of vaccines, this factor favours the US and UK vis-à-vis the EA, which got itself initially into a muddle over vaccines.

With China's real GDP by end-2020 some 8½ per cent above its 2020 average, and 23 per cent up from its 2020 Q1 nadir, the advantage in EMs has lain with China's suppliers. Apart from the energy/commodity price upswings that are benefiting 'commodity countries' this means countries in the region, notably the tech suppliers in Korea and Taiwan.

The implications of this are examined in the next section, but two points can be made here. First, it is ironic that China, the clear source of Covid-19 (despite its strenuous denials), has so far gained significantly vis-à-vis the US and the West in general

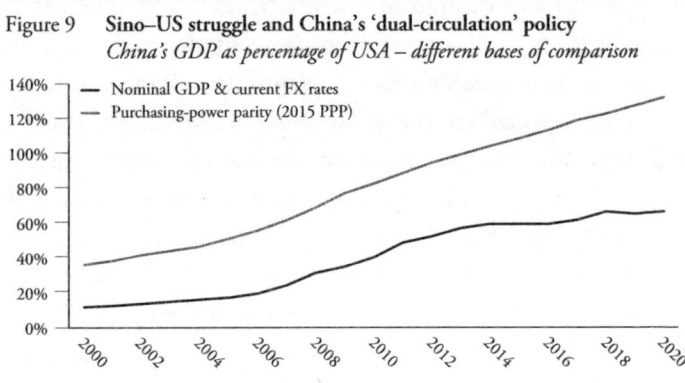

Figure 9 Sino–US struggle and China's 'dual-circulation' policy
China's GDP as percentage of USA – different bases of comparison

from the crisis. Second, China's policy mix was doubly debt intensive: both bank forbearance on the monetary side and the deficit-financed infrastructure programme added to debt totals in the economy. Total non-financial debt in the economy rose from around 250 per cent of GDP in 2017–19 to 290 per cent in 2020 Q3 (Figure 8, page 17). One result is that China's policy is now entering a much more restrictive phase that will inhibit its growth during 2021, though at least consumer spending should become more balanced, as service sectors recover.

While the trade war was initiated by the US in 2018, China's relatively benign experience of the Covid-19 crisis has morphed into an aggressive strategy to win the resulting struggle for world economic (and political and even military) primacy. This is going to be a dominant theme indefinitely. China has responded to the opportunities arising from the 'Trump effect' – broadly, a sense in the world of affairs that US nationalism is inimical to international cooperation. Quickly after the election of President Biden on 3 November, China finalised roping a large portion of the key Asian economies into its Regional Comprehensive Economic Partnership (RCEP) – in effect implementing the Trans-Pacific Partnership rejected by Trump and including long-standing US allies Australia, New Zealand, Japan and Korea (and effectively Taiwan, whose separate existence from China is not acknowledged by Beijing) plus the 'Asian tigers' and Asean countries. Nominally centred in Vietnam, the RCEP agreement was signed on 15 November, 2020, twelve days after the US elections.

China followed this up on 30 December by signing the EU–China Comprehensive Agreement on Investment, not least at the urging of Germany, which had the EU presidency in the second half of 2020. Germany has benefited from booming sales to China for the fifteen-plus years since it became ultra-competitive on costs – courtesy of pre-euro inflationary habits in the rest of the EA – while China's imports and heavy-industrial needs have soared. But the new soft tone of cooperation between the EU and China is also strongly endorsed by France; and in the EU what the Berlin–Paris axis wants, the Berlin–Paris axis gets. To be sure, modifications to this pact will be made as a result of the European Parliament's objections, but something like it will probably prevail. EU countries will turn a blind eye to China's human rights abuses. 'Constructive ambiguity', the phrase used to describe US policy towards Israeli nuclear weapons and China's claim to Taiwan, will be key.

China has launched its 'wolf diplomacy' over its Hong Kong and Xinjiang policies (towards the Uighers) – and potentially

Taiwan, despite the near-monopoly of Taiwan in the global shortage of integrated circuits (chips), which may help protect it for now, as may the sheer difficulty of any attempted conquest. China now seems ready to cut off its market from any country that does not play by its rules, though this is tempered by pragmatism in the US case. Bullying Australia has been quickly followed by sanctions against Europeans protesting about its human rights policies. How likely is the EU to take stands on principle against this? Given the dependence on exports of all European countries, not very.

This raises the issue of a neologism, 'cake-ism' – so named by my colleague Christopher Granville after Boris Johnson's claim that Britain's negotiating strategy vis-à-vis a post-Brexit free trade agreement was to 'have our cake and eat it'. (The original idea is better expressed as to 'eat one's cake and have it' though the Johnson formulation has long been the normal way of putting it.) Arguably, the original cake-ist was General de Gaulle, when he took France out of Nato in 1966. While ostensibly he was expressing doubts about US readiness to use nuclear weapons to defend Europe, particularly West Germany, he made his move knowing that US protection of Europe under Nato had West Germany as the front line. A US conflict with the Soviet Union under Nato would thus protect France anyhow, by dint of geography.

Cake-ism has become important again in the new cold war, the Sino–US struggle for world primacy. The most significant practitioners so far are the Pacific-rim states, notably Japan, Korea and Taiwan, which are part of the China-centred, regional economic bloc but still benefit, as they have since World War

II and the early-1950s Korean War, from US military and strategic alliances. These Pacific-rim countries, as well as south-east Asian countries also now members of the RCEP, have certain advantages that could enable them to get away with cake-ism for quite a while. For Korea and Taiwan, the bargaining power of their prowess in chip production is a major protective factor, but for the whole region the US ambition to continue to project military power in the western Pacific – if only to preserve the free flow of world trade from Chinese forces – will yield for the region's US allies cake-ist leverage to preserve their US alliances while continuing to benefit from trade with China.

How about Europe? To be sure, the threat from Russia can still be conjured up, not least as Putin clearly hankers after reintegrating the Ukraine, which now includes territory that was once part of Poland and Slovakia. But Germany's determined pursuit of the trans-Baltic Nord Stream 2 gas-pipeline project, in the face of multiple objections from the US, is one result of the Trump–Merkel tensions of recent years that may reinforce any sense of indifference the US may feel towards Europe's strategic concerns. Europe is of course protected from direct contact with China by the huge buffer of Russia and the Turkic 'Stans'. US hostility to Russia itself is now almost vestigial, less visceral than in the cold war, despite the recent concerns with Russia-based hackers.

Quite apart from these issues of principle, the fact that European countries spend so little on their own defence rankles with US policymakers. And the European Central Bank's policy of generating several years of beggar-my-neighbour devaluation to offset Europe's domestic demand weakness is another reason for the US to conclude, in the newly fragmented regional-bloc world, that in the graphic early-1990s words about the Balkans of James Baker, George Bush senior's secretary of state, 'We ain't got no dog in that fight' – this new fight being about China's fairly brutal dismissal of the European Parliament's scruples, even though the US, in the form of Biden's secretary of state Antony Blinken, has expressed similar scruples in meetings with Chinese officials.

Maybe Biden feels that Blinken's harsh words about China are enough for now to clarify that post-Trump America is not suddenly going to soften its anti-Chinese stance, though the US administration has been adding to the export bans of certain Chinese firms that were started under Trump. Chiefly though, the new, fragmented world risks being economically inhospitable to export-dependent Europe, especially Germany, whose dependence on exports to China is largest – and most vulnerable anyhow over the next three to five years to China's dual circulation policies of import substitution and increased economic self-reliance.

The analysis in this book in any case concludes that Europe needs a major injection of domestic demand, and that the best way to achieve that will be for Germany to embark on an emergency programme to combat climate change. Many of the advances needed will be engineering solutions, and the Germans are first-class engineers. But the time lags necessary for this to be launched and become operative, even on the most optimistic assumptions, mean that Germany could for the indefinite future continue to be 'soft on China' in the view of political analysts, and that EU governance will avoid confrontation by

Figure 10 **Shares of Chinese GDP**
percentage 1999–2019

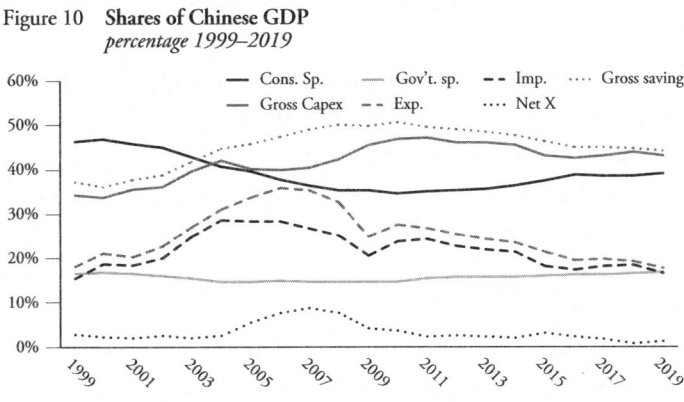

accepting Chinese terms in the bulk of its economic relationships. So the EU is unlikely to take the US side in the Sino–US conflict – at least for now, though both the US and China could try to force it to take sides fairly soon.

One notable point arising from Figure 10 is the declining ratio of imports to China's GDP, from 28.4 per cent at the 2004–06 peak to 16.6 per cent in 2019. The significance of and prospects for this are discussed below. But despite this decline, countries have good reason to curry favour with China over imports. Specifically, while fast growth meant 2020's real GDP was three times 2006's (up 190 per cent), imports were up in real terms by more than three quarters over those fourteen years, despite their falling share of this bounty. But on the general principle of backing winners, and with no other major importing market growing at anywhere near this rate, it makes sense for exporters to strengthen trading and investment links with China.

How does the dual circulation policy affect this? First, it is worth noting that China's import ratio is abnormally high for an economy of its size and extremely large population. The import ratios of the US and Japan, also large, populous countries, are in the region of 15 per cent of GDP. The falling import ratio in this sense simply means China is becoming a less abnormal economy. (Given that the relatively high real FX rate since the GFC ought to have swollen the tendency to import, the most that can be attributed to the FX factor is that imports, though falling back, have done so by less than exports – shown by the near-disappearance of net exports in the twelve years from 2007 to 2019.)

But while the main decline in China's import propensity may have happened already, it is still important that one of the purposes of the dual circulation strategy is import substitution. In general, there are two chief aspects to China's economic strategy. The first is to get away from the emphasis on ultra-polluting 'metal-bashing' that has been central to China's explosive growth over the past thirty to forty years. On the demand side this means less emphasis on capex and industrial exports, and more on a larger share for consumer spending, which is still (miserably) less than 40 per cent of GDP. (As long as consumers are so badly served by the Chinese economy, it will be meaningless to compare its size with the US on a comparable-price, purchasing power parity – PPP – basis.) On the supply side, the strategy means beefing up tech and services, and downgrading heavy industry.

Over time, China's economy will have to become a lot more

consumer orientated. This means the comparison of total GDP (page 24) has to be handled with care. For example, factoring in China's population – at 1.34 billion, 4.3 times the US 311 million – its real GDP per head at PPP (i.e. at comparable prices across the whole economy) was 28 per cent of the US in 2020. But if we allow that some 70 per cent of US GDP is a direct benefit to people, i.e. consumer spending, versus less than 40 per cent of China's, this ratio comes down from 28 per cent to 16 per cent in terms of the economy's real benefit to the people. The distortion of PPP arises from China's 'immobile' service-sector prices being far below those in the US (e.g. haircuts are much cheaper than in New York or LA even in Shanghai and Beijing, let alone remote regions). But the PPP elevation of China's per capita GDP is almost exactly offset by the distortion from China's inadequate consumer spending. So the current-FX version of China's relative GDP, which is 17 per cent of the US on a per-head basis, looks more realistic. And on that basis China's economy is still only 75 per cent of the US, and even with growth of 5 per cent and 2 per cent respectively, may not match the US until 2030.

The second major Chinese goal is a tech sector to rival the US. Until recently Chinese tech was heavily dependent on imported supplies and purloined intellectual property, mostly American, though it is now less so in significant sectors, such as artificial intelligence. In a sense relentlessly mid-tech, China's Baidus and Tencents are highly profitable, but mostly on the back of a protected home market of 1.3 billion people, rather than any cutting-edge technical merits. It is open to question what chance of major success a top-down, *dirigiste* economic policy has at the tech frontier. This appears to be the weakest aspect of China's strategy – the country will probably become the genuinely largest world economy, but that may not be enough for true economic leadership.

It remains open to question if China will prove able to generate its own cutting-edge tech products, particularly at the highest standards at the tech frontier. So its first priority in the dual circulation policy of import substitution is de-Americanisation. Big beneficiaries of this strategy are tech firms in Korea and Taiwan (and Japan, though proportionately less). But Chinese growth will slow sharply during 2021, not least because its macro-policies have generated a double whammy of debt escalation: bank forbearance ultimately means losses that will be charged to the government, adding to debt escalation resulting from the budget deficits arising from funding the 2020 infrastructure programme with debt. And as Chinese (and Western) consumers return to service consumption, goods exporters and producers, notably China itself, German-centred Europe and Japan, will tend to feel the draught.

The danger for the likes of German-centred Europe in all this is that the natural fallback of Chinese goods demand in future years may be reinforced by import substitution under the dual-circulation policy. This will be much easier for China to achieve in 'industry' than in cutting-edge tech. So the current benign combination of Chinese consumers avoiding service consumption (e.g. foreign travel) and buying cars to avoid crowded public transport, together with China's import substitution being focused on US tech products is unlikely to outlast 2021. Dependence on exports to China is thus a potential weakness.

The post-Covid world economy

Before looking at the longer-term features of the Sino–US cold war some points must be raised about the post-Covid world economy, quite apart from its reinforcement of the fragmentation discussed above. Has growth been permanently damaged? Or can we just spring back once C-19 vaccines are fully deployed and credibly efficacious? The damage, after all, arose from measures to check the pandemic not from deep-seated structural or financial problems weakening the supply-side potential of economies. There has also been no cyclical problem with overheating and/or inflation (typical causes of recessions) – quite the contrary, as the Covid-19 recession resulted from a collapse of demand. While the lasting effects of Covid-19 on medium- or even long-term growth potential are highly uncertain, some things are becoming clear.

First, the substantial damage that has been done is concentrated in a few service sectors. Hospitality and entertainment have been badly hit, as has travel, notably airlines and hotels. While vaccines may permit revival of these businesses, there may be longer-term damage, and certainly many high-street businesses (main-street in US parlance) have been forced to close. Reopening may require substantial recapitalisation, and for some proprietors the experience may have been stressful enough, either financially or in terms of general anxiety, to make them give up for good.

It is far from clear that vaccinations will permit a 'return to normal' in such matters as sports events, cinemas (and theatres), and even restaurants and bars. It is not just that lockdowns have caused much associational activity to be prohibited. Consumers have become in many cases cautious and inhibited by requirements like wearing masks. In China, for example, though the authorities make much of having got the disease under control, people have not gone back to previous levels of service consumption. US consumers are more gung-ho, but in Europe new Covid-19 waves have led to renewed lockdowns, with the EU's vaccination programme initially in disarray and political leaders not above stoking fears on nationalist grounds. Though this disarray is being sorted, the fear of new Covid-19 variants and mutations is likely to inhibit associational spending for at least a year or two.

The return to normal

In Britain people are heaving a sigh of relief, anticipating a Covid-vaccinated return to normal. In the US restrictions have been lifted for months, and in many instances (e.g. Texas) were never much anyhow, to no particular disadvantage vis-à-vis for instance California. Even in continental Europe problems relating to the mismanaged vaccine programme are giving way to rapid recovery. While India has witnessed distressing scenes, this is gradually giving way to India's new prosperity, as for the past thirty to forty years, assuming it can recover from the huge damage wrought by successive waves of Covid-19.

There's only one snag: the new normal will not be the old normal. There are some permanent changes resulting from the Covid-19 crisis of 2020, but also major alterations in the outlook of consumers and the policy environment. What are the prospects for commuting, continued working from home, and business travel? Will consumers even *want* to return to previous levels of eating out, drinking in bars or even attendance at sports and cultural events? And what about holiday travel? Has the lavish adoption of easy fiscal and monetary policies changed the outlook for interest rates and inflation? And what about the huge increment of debt in 2020?

WFH is here to stay

How much fun is it really, pushing on to a crowded train five days a week? At an April webinar TS Lombard conducted some polls of the clients in (virtual) attendance. The results of the two polls on travel are shown in Figures 11 and 12 (pages 36 and 38). A 13 per cent minority hard core predicted that we'll be back to commuting five days a week soon, but 87 per cent said 1–3 days a week, with no votes for 'Seldom, if at all'. Earlier this year, the heads of Goldman Sachs and JP Morgan said they expect a full return to five-days-a week commuting. But is this realistic? For those aspiring to be the next head of the firm (or even to get there eventually) the answer may well be 'Yes'. It is no accident that JP Morgan supplies all its employees with a 'free lunch' every day – in defiance of economists who say there is no such thing! That free lunch has kept noses as close to the grindstone as managers might hope, but is it enough to induce employees to spend up to two hours a day crowded together on a commute that they have just spent twelve months finding to be unnecessary?

And what about that zero vote for 'Seldom, if at all'? At TS Lombard in London three employees out of thirty are

Figure 11 TS Lombard webinar poll

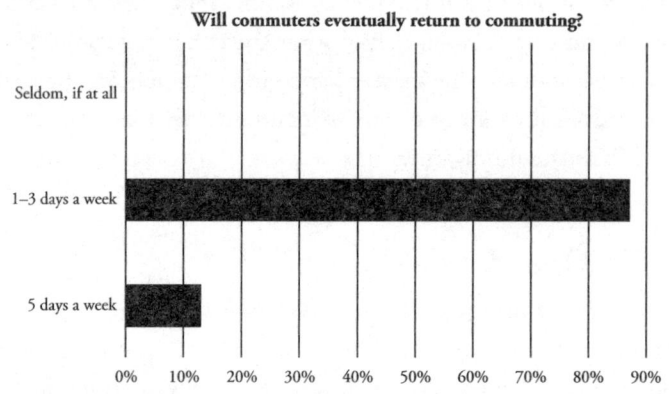

Sources: TS Lombard

over seventy. They will in future be commuting seldom, if at all. Video conferencing may not help much when it comes to getting to know new employees, but it works fine for most of the day-to-day talking needed with people we already know well. And what about the three other employees that want in future to live, respectively, in Switzerland, Sheffield and Edinburgh? How often will they be commuting? Maybe seldom, if at all? So maybe Goldman and JP Morgan will be the exceptions. Reader comments on the press reports of their heads' assertions about returning to a full five-day commute used the word 'dinosaurs', as well as mentioning how having a limousine and driver makes commuting a lot less unattractive. Although there was no mention of King Canute acknowledging his inability to turn the tide back, it is a fair comparison – except that Canute was accepting reality, unlike the two bank heads: to be fair, it is more likely that they felt this five-day-commute policy would enable them to steal a march on the banking competition.

Already, the housing market is responding to the new prevalence of WFH. A lot of people live in homes that are ill suited to WFH. The dining-room table is fine if you have a dining room, but many do not, especially in crowded city flats or apartments. Of course, this is a factor that may drive people back to the office. But it is also driving an urge to improve the home, to accommodate a future in which WFH is the norm or at least normal. And then there are the wilder spirits who, in the US context, want to live in the Adirondacks not just commute from suburban Westchester – maybe in Britain the Scottish Highlands not just Edinburgh. And what about the ultras? People who can WFH from the cold north ... and then spend the northern winter on a beach close to the equator or even in South America. Holiday hotels, after a tough year, will give them a good deal. WFH does not necessarily mean working from home – all you need is reliable WiFi and you can work from anywhere!

Of course we don't know – the new working 'social contract' will take years to emerge. But over years we can expect the most radical solution to be the ultimate result, if only for cost savings. Much the same applies to business travel (see Figure 12, overleaf). How will finance directors behave, now that we've gone a year with virtually no business travel? 'Essential' will have to prove itself, and 'nice to have' may be sucking wind (unless it's the boss, of course, or the boss's spouse). The pressure for cost savings will be relentless. If bosses do not trust WFH employees to work, they will find ways of monitoring what they are up to.

Figure 12   TS Lombard webinar poll

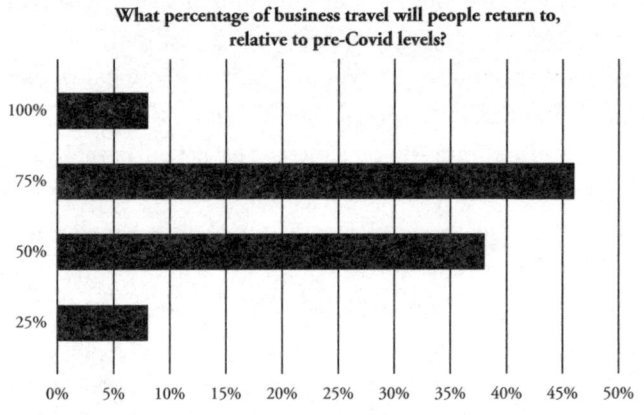

Sources: TS Lombard

And the sheer pleasantness of WFH without commuting should encourage compliance (with young children away at school in contrast to some tiresome Covid-19 lockdowns).

The original argument for mobile phones (back in the 1990s) was that when you called someone, you wanted to talk to that person, not to whoever might answer at whatever place their landline phone happened to be located. That argument was won well before smartphones came in, yet mobiles (cell phones in the US) are still able to charge much more than landline phones – the product is clearly superior. What has this to do with business travel? Well … how desperate to see you is your client – really? Maybe they'd prefer to tell you what they want, and when they want it, rather than have you just turn up to sell to them.

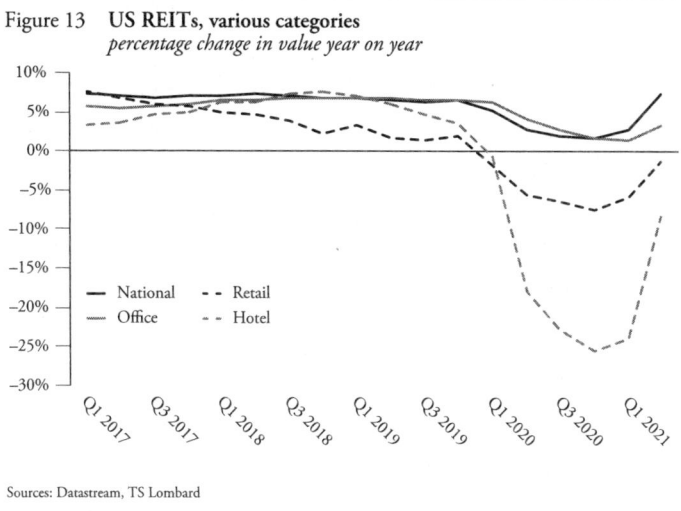

Figure 13 **US REITs, various categories**
percentage change in value year on year

Sources: Datastream, TS Lombard

Figure 13 (above) shows year on year valuation changes for US REITs (real estate investment trusts). While the mature development of online shopping shows up in the fall-off of shop properties, the shock effect of Covid-19 and WFH on office property values has yet to register – hardly at all, let alone fully. REIT investors must have deep belief in pronouncements by the heads of Goldman and JP Morgan. But they could well be underestimating the long-term pressure on costs from finance directors – they may overstate the potential savings, but will be encouraged by the fifteen months for which commuting and business travel has been severely curtailed. Maybe urban real estate has passed a tipping point. Fully serviced offices may win out over traditional city-centre leases, and people wanting relief from the home environment may prefer a local serviced office to a long commute to centralised offices.

Compare the performance of hotel REITs. Our client poll suggested a 25–50 per cent cut in business travel, and hotel REITs are down by a quarter: a quick question-and-answer by means of Zoom may take care of what you previously had to travel for. Certainly, finance directors will be happier that way. Probably our client voters were underestimating the likely fall in business travel in favour of video conferencing. A full year's demonstration that we can do without much of it is a red rag to the bull vis-à-vis management cost cutters. They will wear down the wannabe travellers at the expense of air travel and high-class hotels.

When it comes to travel for pleasure and vacations, the outlook is not so bleak. But even this silver lining has a cloud behind it. Who keeps air travel cheap? The answer, apart from specialist cheapo merchants like Ryanair and EasyJet, is business travellers paying for premium seats: first class, business class or full-price transferable economy. Cut down their contribution and the number of flights will be less and, more importantly, the cost will go up for passengers in 'the back of the bus'. Nobody knows at this point how big the decline in pleasure travel will be, but the new normal will be less than before.

Inflation? Not yet! Recapitalisation? Yes!

What does reopening mean? For consumers it means we can go back to restaurants and bars to enjoy ourselves again. And we have had several months of below-par spending, with consumer

Figure 14 **Broad money growth, three-month moving average**
percentage year on year

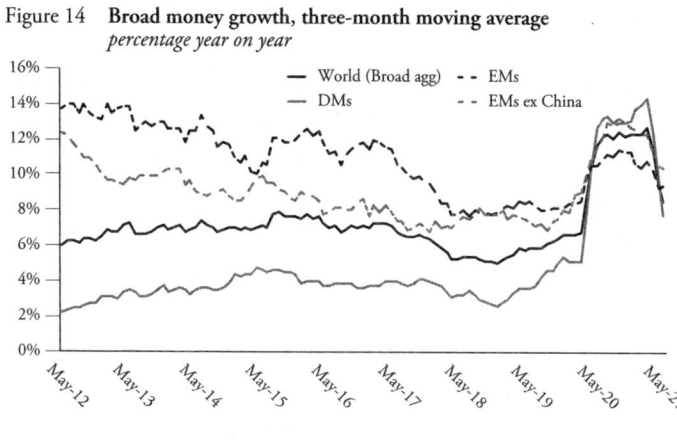

Sources: Datastream, TS Lombard

saving rates well above normal as a result. Meanwhile, central banks have been pumping out liquidity as never before – by general consent, advanced-country recovery failed in 2009–19 and policymakers are anxious to avoid repeating their mistakes.

When spare cash meets financially stressed business, the first result is higher prices. In a pub immediately after they were allowed to reopen, interviewing a person looking for career advice, two pints of bitter and two of Guinness cost thirty pounds. Bitter from up-market Waitrose costs five pounds for two litres – at which rate those pub drinks would have come to less than six pounds. It was sunny, but viciously cold for 1 May, and the reopening rules meant drinking outside. Much as I love a pint in a pub, this author at least can and will wait till the price gouging stops. It was a nice pub in a smart part of London, but a recent outdoor lunch in an undistinguished restaurant was similarly overpriced, at least compared to reasonable pre-Covid prices. Maybe lockdown has taught me lessons: service consumption is expensive, even with gig-economy labour.

Much is made of the surge of liquidity sponsored by central banks both in driving stock markets higher and as a potential cause of inflation. But the story of price gouging by restaurants and bars may have a different message: small service businesses have to make up for months of slow business and inadequate revenues. In effect, many street-level businesses may need to recapitalise themselves. A first reaction as they reopen may be to charge like a rhinoceros, but the reaction of potential consumers may thwart their hopes, slowing the recovery. It is entirely possible that the surge of liquidity will prove to be needed to finance recapitalisation, assisted (as regards ownership in street-level service businesses) by the stock-market boost that the liquidity has already provided. Recovery and inflation, i.e. street-level service recovery, may only phase in over years, and for businesses depending on commuters – lunchtime sandwich bars or business-district restaurants – perhaps never.

Figure 15 (opposite) shows the May 2021 US economic forecast of TS Lombard. Any forecast in these circumstances is bound to be a shot in the dark. A major point is that Q1 was held back by substantial liquidation of inventory to 6.4 per cent growth (at a quarterly annual rate, the normal way of presenting such data in the US). A further upward bounce in Q2 growth was therefore nearly certain. The 9.5 per cent Q2 number in the chart does not depend on a big export surge, which could ensure an even higher number than that.

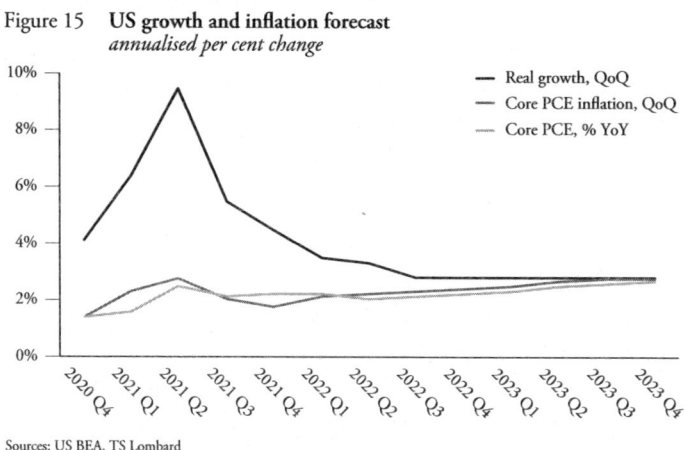

Figure 15 **US growth and inflation forecast**
annualised per cent change

Sources: US BEA, TS Lombard

It is important to note the forecast of an inflation *slow-down* during Q3–Q4 (i.e. the quarter-to-quarter rate, not the year-on-year rate). The time lag in core inflation behind real activity is understated by the usual belief that it is one year; eighteen months is more like it. This forecast is consistent with the view that we have passed a key point in the evolution of policy cycles – towards readier adoption of Keynesian deficits rather than the monetarist monopoly prevailing since 1980. This almost inevitably implies a medium-term inflation problem, but this is much more likely (given lagged responses) in 2023–24 than any time this year or even next, when quarter-on-quarter inflation should start to accelerate on our forecast.

The bond market has got it back to front on inflation. Its two-year view of inflation is unduly high, misunderstanding current price jumps (and rapidly rising energy and commodity prices) for an upcycle of inflation. Even the five-year view (2½ per cent for the consumer price index) may depend on energy being in a 'commodity supercycle', which is unlikely. There is no supercycle, nor is there likely to be – there is a cycle, but it isn't super – a typical journalistic exaggeration. A supercycle is one that sees commodities barely cool off in between two big upward legs.

There have been two commodity supercycles in the past fifty years (Figure 16, opposite). The first was in 1973–80, and reflected the fact that while major advanced-country inflation had set in from the late-1960s, oil prices remained stable: they were thus falling in real terms. The Yom Kippur War and the Arab oil boycott spurred soaring oil prices and a commodity supercycle, which peaked in 1980, when Paul Volcker's tight money wrung inflation out of the system.

The second supercycle similarly followed declining real oil prices, as the late-1990s Asian crisis came to dominate the global industrial cycle, lowering oil prices below ten dollars per barrel by the end of 1998. China exploding on to the world economy then maintained its real growth at a double-figure rate (despite the GFC) until 2011, the 'true' peak despite 2008's temporary spike – Olympics driven? After 2011, oil prices remained in the $110 region until 2014, partly through lagged responses (inertia) and partly owing to supply-side constraints (Arab Spring, Iran sanctions, etc.).

The commodities that can inflate a lot over the next two to three years are anyhow not energy so much as metals. They are already included in the US 'core deflator', which is forecast to

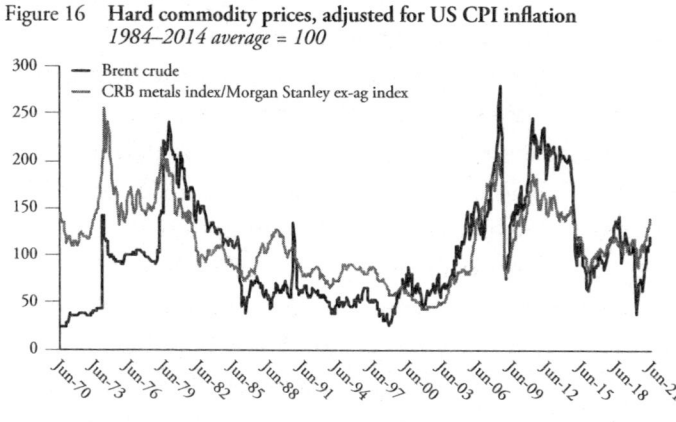

Figure 16   **Hard commodity prices, adjusted for US CPI inflation**
1984–2014 average = 100

Sources: Datastream, TS Lombard

slow a little in the latter half of 2021. As the global recovery this year shifts focus on to service spending, the recent commodity upcycle could run out of steam. Market investors find it hard to understand that the economy moves with major lagged effects – responses and adjustments to new facts are not immediate, as they are in financial markets. If and when the Commodity Research Bureau industrials sub-index is changed to include battery minerals and rare earths, the bond market may well be expecting 2½–3 per cent inflation. But by then it will already be 2023–24, perhaps later.

Recent evidence shows that the all-up cost of wind/solar electricity fell through that of coal/gas-generated electricity in 2018; the oil price cycle (down, then up) driven by the Covid-19 crisis has masked this. Biden's reinsertion of the US into 2015's

Paris accords on climate change has spurred a recent global rush to make strong commitments to reducing greenhouse gas emissions by 2030 – with net zero promised in many countries by 2050, though China, the largest source of CO_2 emissions (29 per cent of the world total in 2019) is only committed to net zero by 2060. The development of cheap electricity from wind power and solar panels means that the forthcoming decade could see widespread obsolescence – so-called stranded assets – in the energy systems of advanced countries and China, whose hangover of traditional heavy industry sees it still building new coal-fired power stations. The attention-grabbing car industry is already well on the way to electrification, which means major investment is needed in on-the-road battery-charging facilities, alongside retirement of newly obsolete power-generating assets.

Long-term growth decline – but big opportunities

As described above, the Covid-19 crisis has reinforced the tendency towards regional economic blocs, as well as fostering outright nationalism. When it comes to potential growth in North America and Europe, the US is gaining from the surge of tech activity provoked by Covid-19, which in a period of months triggered changes that might otherwise have taken several years to be implemented. It also provoked the kind of management rethink that could produce a tipping point in implementation of these changes, as well as possible cost savings, as outlined above in discussing commuters and office attendance.

While the US may find that such tech-based productivity increases match or even outweigh the losses from global fragmentation, for Europe that will be unlikely, with the leading tech-industry firms heavily concentrated in America. In Europe export dependence potentially curtails growth prospects in a fragmenting world with less intercontinental trade. China may continue on its path of catch-up growth, as its GDP per capita is realistically less than a fifth of the US; its goal of tech independence from the US may prove harder to achieve than it supposes in its plans. But Europe and EMs not relating strongly to the US and/or China are significantly threatened in future growth potential.

Quite a lot more worrying than the immediate effects of Covid-19 is the apparently total dependence of both the US and Europe on budget deficits to generate growth. Figure 17 (overleaf) shows why debt ratios have been increasing over the years – up in recessions, but with no offsetting declines in years of good growth. The shift last year to willing use of fiscal stimulus in both the US and Europe is probably essential to future advanced-country growth, and it seems the US is moving from forty years of trusting the private sector to the kind of managed capitalism that prevailed from Franklin Delano Roosevelt to Richard Nixon. This puts a very different gloss on the post-Covid return to normal, which becomes almost historic!

What the budget-deficit chart also explains is why Europe has had to adopt negative real (and nominal) interest rates, while the US has not – at least in nominal rates. The US government has just been that much more willing to borrow. But Figure 18 (overleaf) shows the steady decline in economic growth in the G7. The US looks better managed in the short and long term, but even the US trend is downward. What is the meaning of

Figure 17 **Structural, i.e. cyclically adjusted, budget balances**
percentage of GDP

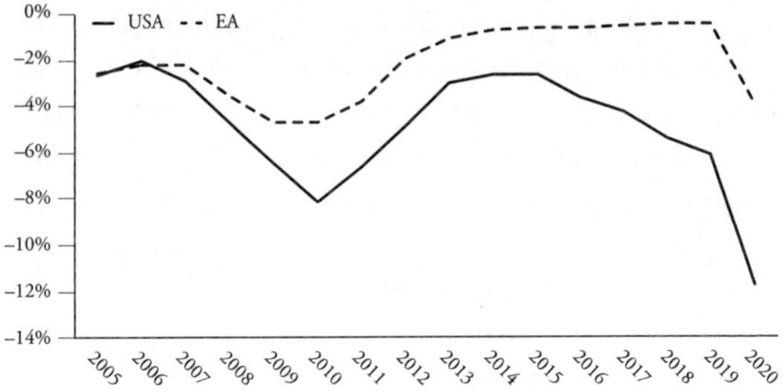

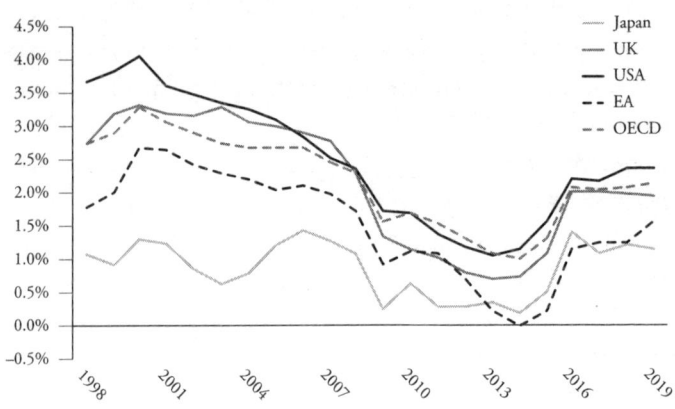

Sources: OECD, TS Lombard

Figure 18 **Real GDP growth, pre-Covid, 7-year moving averages**
% p.a.

Sources: OECD, TS Lombard

this dearth of domestic demand that has to be made up by government deficits? It is true that capital inflows to the US come close to matching its budget deficits, but much of that capital flow reflects interest rate differences that are the product of the differences in deficits, rather than the stock-market attractions of US tech investment (for example). But the real interest-rate differentials probably do reflect negligible or even negative real returns on capital in continental Europe and Japan.

Contrary to popular supposition, Karl Marx was a great admirer of the dynamism of capitalism (as well he might have been in the second quarter of the nineteenth century), but he did suggest a shortage of demand might be typical in a mature capitalist economy. (This was quite a widespread conjecture at the time.) Is this the problem we now have? Does the private sector's desire to save exceed profitable capex opportunities? If so, government debt levels rising may be the mechanism for the Rogoff/Reinhart effect of slowing economic growth. The chart on various cycles' seven-year-average growth also shows the OECD's estimate of potential growth. But this is a supply-side measure. If the demand is not there, only rising government debt levels will ensure the potential growth occurs. And sooner or later excessive debts could cause financial crisis and write-offs. Japan has avoided this so far, but the toll on its growth has been severe. The major risk to long-run growth prospects from rising government debt ratios is analysed on pages 60–62.

The Marxian danger of fundamental demand shortfalls gains strength from an entirely different perspective – that of Frank Ramsey in 1928. His theory of savings broadly concluded that (relative to future contingent needs) we do not save enough.

But suppose (as argued in the Introduction – see page 3) that we sense we are not saving enough. Alongside saving, the rate of investment is driven by the development of profitable investment opportunities in business. It is axiomatic that investment equals saving, when measured *ex post*. But a sense that we are not saving (or have not saved) enough could cause the *ex ante* desire to save to exceed the supply of good entrepreneurial profitable investment opportunities. (There is no connection in principle between the scale of profit opportunities and people's aggregated desire for saving.) In that case, with *ex ante* saving tending to exceed *ex ante* investment, demand could consistently fall short, in a sort of permanent liquidity trap. This would also go some way towards explaining both the prevalence of budget deficits (filling in the demand deficiency) and the parallel decline of both real growth and interest rates (both nominal and real).

The allusion in the Introduction to the recent fall in the all-up cost of electricity from renewable sources (solar and wind) below that of conventional, coal- and gas-generated power could therefore turn out to be crucial for future long-run growth. It may well prove, and certainly in Europe, that the investment potential of this will be a key source of badly needed future demand, with sunny Africa and South America as highly profitable locations. This prospect is independent of the 'war' on climate change, as renewables-sourced electricity is already cheaper and due to become more so. Just as post-World War II rebuilding in 1948–73, reinforced by baby-boom demographics, was a spur to a quarter-century boom, so the electrification of the global south may provide the impetus for future long-run growth, ironically supplying the profit that Marx thought capitalism would lack.

Inflation as a later long-term threat

Dealing with climate change is just one reason why the medium-term recovery of demand could be strong, so that the bond market's worries about inflation have solid grounding. In a transition away from monetarist-monopoly policies, budget deficits may also presage inflation. A little-publicised feature of the advance report on US Q1 GDP was a 28 per cent increase in government spending in just one quarter (i.e. from 2020 Q4: the actual quarter-on-quarter rate, not an annual rate). The February fiscal stimulus was its chief cause, including one-off payments of $1,400 to many people. The effect on the total government budget deficit (including social security as well as state and local governments) is shown in Figure 19 overleaf (the deficit is referred to as 'negative net lending'). Of course, 2020 Q3 was a big deficit quarter, but it seemed likely in the autumn that the deficit would come down naturally as the Covid-19 relief payments became less needed and fell away. The data are not yet in for part of the receipts of government, but the quarterly increase in the deficit is $½ trillion ($2 trillion annualised, as in Figure 19), and if this is added to the going rate of deficit during 2019 ($1½ trillion) the likely underlying, cyclically adjusted rate will be $2 trillion or more, 10 per cent of GDP.

What these numbers suggest include the following points.

- TS Lombard forecasts that real growth will remain at 2¾

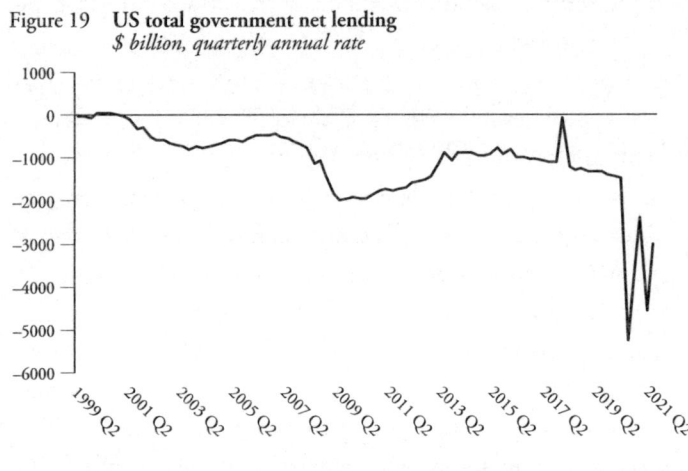

Figure 19 **US total government net lending**
$ billion, quarterly annual rate

Sources: US BEA, TS Lombard

per cent through 2023, surpassing its pre-Covid trend in mid-2022 so that overheating develops and then intensifies during 2023.

- Inflation could accelerate to a similar, 2¾ per cent rate. Continually increased overheating despite the budget deficit being shrunk somewhat by the recovery (as tax revenues revive and relief spending lapses) suggests the Federal Reserve's desire for core inflation to average 2 per cent, including the below-2 per cent results in 2019–21, will be met in 2023–24.
- Whatever happens to medium-term inflation – maybe the Fed will tighten in response to inflation meeting its target and *real* interest rates could go up – a positive *real* ten-year

US Treasury yield with inflation prospectively 2¾ per cent in 2023 would be 3 per cent or more.
- Fed policy of aiming for inflation above 2 per cent to compensate for several years of it having been below the 2 per cent target could be 'successful' quite soon, testing the Fed's mandate, which includes holding inflation down as well as securing good growth and stable financial conditions.
- Biden may get less of his 'budget-balance-neutral' Families Plan and Jobs Plan than he hopes through Congress, and bells and whistles attached to whatever eventually emerges could well add to the deficit.
- The question of whether government debt/GDP ratios matter will be thoroughly tested. (Advocates of modern monetary theory – MMT – say they do not matter, though Voltaire might have said MMT is neither modern, nor monetary, nor a theory.)

Several factors combine to make significant inflation and higher interest rates likely in the mid-2020s. First, large budget deficits are on the cards as Biden strives to get a strong Democratic vote in the 2022 mid-term elections, learning from Obama's fate after his 2010 mid-term losses. Second, infrastructure capex programmes develop a momentum of their own that can thwart any attempted restraint. Third, a downside scenario is that there could be inhibitions on the US economic recovery that encourage pursuit of expansive policies well into the 2020s but build up the long-run boost to demand. In this context, the inflation caused by interruption of supply chains could threaten a degree of stagflation. And lastly, the task of slowing inflation, once it has generated real momentum, is a lot less easy than central bankers have recently been acknowledging, as shown by the history of the 1980s.

Covid-19 scars – jobs too

Employment has also been damaged, and especially low-paid jobs. This greater inequality is the notorious K-shaped effect (which ignores the vertical, left-hand stroke of a K) of the Covid-19 recession. It has exposed the weakness of the 2009–19 jobs recovery from the GFC, which was heavily concentrated in often casual low-wage jobs typical of hospitality and entertainment – waiters, bartenders, behind-the-scenes hotel workers – not least because that recovery largely depended on monetary-policy stimulus, which depends on the wealth effect of extra spending by the beneficiaries of asset-price gains. In other words, monetarist recovery policy (after the GFC) made the rich richer. Those low-wage jobs, moreover, that remained unaffected by Covid-19 – e.g. nurses, care workers and garbage operatives – have in many cases become a lot more stressful. Office workers who in many cases can work from home have been relatively protected, as well as (for the most part) better paid to start with. Parents with children prevented from going to school – more of a European than an American problem – are under particular stress even if they can work from home (in fact, especially if they can!) and in many cases these are in low-paid jobs.

Surprisingly large numbers of people have proved able to work from home during the Covid-19 crisis, including the majority of desk workers. It is highly unlikely that this will be fully reversed when vaccines enable things to return to normal. This could turn city-centre office property into stranded assets – i.e. obsolescent, just as is threatened for oil reserves. City-centre retail property has been eroded in value for more than twenty years now by online shopping, but Covid-19 has strengthened this trend as people stayed at home more and needed home delivery. City centres will be undergoing radical transformation with the confluence of these two effects. Major planning and zoning rules will need adjustment to enable office and retail space to be transformed into housing. This too will favour growth in the more market-orientated American economy than in regulated (over-regulated?) Europe.

What firms adjusting to WFH have yet had to face up to on any scale is how to integrate new workers into their operations – and simply getting to know them – if many employees are working from home. And given that 'home' simply means somewhere with WiFi, which is what makes WFH possible, the dispersal of people could be a lot more extensive than is implied by moving to the suburbs or the country. Video conferencing has benefited productivity by cutting into the length of some business meetings, one significant gain being that video-conference meetings generally start on time and are shorter than old-style face to face; many of them also have proved less than vital, so the inability to call a meeting has helped reduce time-wasting. Less business travel means airlines and four/five-star hotels are in long-term difficulties, which in the case of airlines was coming anyhow in connection with combating climate change.

Even with rapid vaccine roll-out, this damage will hold output and employment below pre-Covid levels for some time.

It is likely that the US economy will only reach the output level of 2019 Q4 in 2021 Q2, a year and a half later, and in continental Europe that point may be in 2022's first half. China to be sure, exceeded 2019 Q4 in 2020 Q3, using TS Lombard's recalculation of real GDP, and was 23 per cent up in 2020 Q4 from the Q1 low point. But that reflected the special factors already mentioned (pages 21–4) as well as the easier enforcement ability of any dictatorship, as shown by China's early-2020 success in restricting the spread of the disease. For Westerners, a return to old habits such as cinema going or sports events and other entertainment, and even going out to restaurants and bars, may be a long way off, even assuming old habits are eventually fully restored, as is unlikely for commuting.

There is a dilemma here. Full and rapid recovery from the Covid-19 recession will depend on the willingness of governments to continue with lavish deficit spending, and even in China the escalation of debt levels, not just in government, is already shifting the policy emphasis back towards a 'debt brake', as the Germans call it. In 2010 Kenneth Rogoff and Carmen Reinhart published the view that government debt ratios above 90 per cent of GDP would be bad for growth, and though their views (and even their statistical work) have been disputed, the jury is still out on this question, specifically the effect of high and/or rising debt ratios on *real growth* (as opposed to the effects of large debts on financial stability and interest rates, both real and nominal).

Even with Japan's government debt considered net rather than gross – the argument for netting debt ratios being that Japan's government has unusually large financial assets worth

100 per cent of GDP) – Japan remains the most indebted country in the world today. This is challenged by France's soaring business-sector debt, with its total non-financial debt only brought down to Japan's level by government financial assets worth nearly 50 per cent of GDP.

Japan makes a good example of the Rogoff/Reinhart principle: real growth averaged nearly 5 per cent in the years before Japan's bubble burst in 1990, but fell to about 1 per cent between then and the GFC, and has been only about ½ per cent since the GFC. There may be other reasons for this, but its very high debt levels certainly encourage private-sector savings, which are a higher share of incomes even than in German-centred Europe, the other great savings-glut region among advanced economies. The natural response to private savings in excess of capex needs is that the saving has to be offset by government deficits, which raise debt ratios even higher. Without espousing the full Ricardian equivalence idea that budget deficits will cause precautionary saving to increase against future troubles, it is reasonable to think it will add to such excessive precautionary saving. This would increase the future need for budget deficits and implies a vicious upward circle of debt. And the constant desire of finance ministries to limit the escalation of debt tends to ensure fiscal policy strays towards strictness, with serial liquidity traps, as we have seen in Japan.

While slower growth can therefore be plausibly linked to excessive debt levels, the operating principle has been that governments cannot 'go bust' as they have the power of the printing press, by which the currency can be debased if necessary. This is true of the US today and the UK historically – even in the days of the gold standard, a stricter environment than America's with the dollar enjoying the 'exorbitant privilege' of being an unanchored reserve currency. But it is not true for developing countries, which either as countries or in the business sector have large US-dollar debts. Neither is it true of countries in the EA, though attitudes towards debts vary a lot between conservative Germany and free-spending Mediterranean countries (now including France).

So the jury is out on the question of how high debt ratios affect long-term growth rates, and will remain out for many years before conclusions can be reached, if ever. Meanwhile, once recovery to former potential output trends has been achieved, what is the effect of the trade war and the Covid-19 crisis on potential growth? On this point major differences in the likely effect of these two factors (fragmentation and accelerated tech changes) seem clear, favouring America (as well as China, India, and EMs generally) more than export-dependent Europe (and maybe Japan).

US/European divergence

The effects on world growth of the Sino–US trade war are unambiguously negative. By fragmenting the world economy into regional blocs, it has raised costs and lowered the productivity of capital. The trade-war damage to growth and the return on capital has arisen because (for example) an American CEO might site a new plant to supply the firm's needs in Alabama rather than Fujian, for fear of the US president suddenly putting a high tariff on imports. The Covid-19 crisis is reinforcing this shift in priorities towards security of supply, quite apart from the fragmenting effects of greater nationalism, as many global supply chains have been disrupted by Covid-19 lockdowns.

But though Covid-19 has added to fragmentation, its economic effects are not all negative. It has also concentrated into a few months of 2020 tech progress that might otherwise have been spread over several years. And in both WFH and online shopping, it is likely that the stimulus to productivity may have turned into a tipping point, generating productivity gains from reduced commuting and lesser demand for expensive city-centre office space, as well as cost savings in business travel.

With so much of the tech sector located in America, the benefits of the huge increase in tech applications to productivity are likely to be concentrated there, and may well outweigh the loss of growth potential from fragmentation of globalisation – especially if less expensive offices result from reduced worker commuting, as well as a more stringent attitude towards business travel. So Covid-19 may bring the US benefits that offset the trade-war losses, while Europe's more export-dependent countries lose more from the trade war and China's dual-circulation policy (pages 29–30) and gain less from accelerated adoption of tech. China, at the centre of the largest regional bloc, should continue to catch up with advanced countries much as before. But China is unlikely to be able to substitute for its pre-trade-war dependence on US tech, so its rate of catch-up may be slower than before.

The new drab – the greying of society

The Covid-19 crisis has been bad news for 'style'. People largely confined to their homes or working there have not needed to dress smartly, and in many instances have not. Talk of a 'new roaring 20s' seems fanciful, as those best placed by the crisis have been the old, and style leadership is something they have mostly given up, if not grown out of! Maybe the greying of society by population ageing – both lower birth rates and later deaths – will give way to a lively new culture, but here we must look at the economics of ageing.

How are people actually responding to population ageing? It is widely supposed that ageing will cause the dependency ratio to go up, superimposing a shortage of labour on the already inflationary scenario of more people consuming while not producing. But it is far from clear that this is what will happen, and this potential inflation ignores the possible offset of older people selling off assets to fund retirement, with deflationary effect. Several factors at least suggest that a large proportion of people over the official retirement age of sixty-five will increasingly carry on working.

- The chief reason for sixty-five being the retirement age is that many jobs involve physical strain which an older person cannot sustain. But the proportion of such jobs is now much smaller than before, enabling increasing numbers of people to continue to work after that age.
- Life expectancy is improving. Sayings like 'Seventy is the new fifty' may exaggerate older people's capacity for work, but without doubt it is rising.

- State pensions are relatively ungenerous, having in many instances been designed to avoid dire poverty rather than support continued old-age affluence.

In terms of population decline, the leading example is Japan, where population growth has stalled over the past ten years, and the over-sixty-fives have gone up to 32 per cent from 26 per cent. Over the same time, the proportion of over-sixty-fives still in the labour force has gone up to 25 per cent from 20 per cent, and among 65–69s to 50 per cent from 38 per cent. (The over-seventies ratio is up too, to 17½ per cent from 13 per cent.) One hears many stories about elderly Japanese retraining as plumbers, but the numbers speak for themselves without resort to anecdotes.

Traditional life-cycle analysis suggests that the personal savings rate will decline in an ageing population, as older people liquidate assets to fund retirement. But older people continuing to work, partly to make up for small public pensions and inadequate saving earlier in life, will tend to save. Thus in Japan, despite personal savings rates well above 10 per cent of disposable income until the early 1990s, the personal savings rate decline (as large pre-World War II population cohorts retired) bottomed out at around 3 per cent just before 2007–09's GFC. It rose to nearly 6 per cent by 2019, even though earlier in the post-GFC decade it was depressed by an ill-judged attempt at fiscal austerity in the form of a consumption tax increase.

Older people working and saving undermines the longer-term case for budget balancing by governments. One of the better arguments for budgetary austerity has for a long time been that an ageing population will impose inflationary strains on the economy. But if a rising proportion of older people are working, keeping up the supply of labour and saving, so that demand is falling vis-à-vis supply, inflationary strains are unlikely or at most moderate.

In this long-term fiscal context, the revenue from the carbon tax proposed in Essay 2 would threaten fiscal deflation, which we had too much of anyhow in 2011–19. An offset to this would include welfare payments to compensate for the regressive impact of the tax and/or tax cuts. The need for a welfare offset is assumed here, shifting the focus on to which taxes to cut and the structure of taxation in general. Of course, the future is unknown, and this analysis may turn out not to apply; some degree of long-run fiscal rigour, or austerity, may be needed. But in that case levying a carbon tax, even with allowance for welfare offsets for the poor, will put governments in a strong fiscal position.

Short-term policy post-Covid19

A lot of (metaphorical) ink has been spilt warning us that governments will have their work cut out to balance the budget in future years when, as is likely, the economy has recovered from the Covid-19 crisis. The message of this book is that they would be unwise to try for at least two major reasons.

- Most of the emergency subsidies to deal with the crisis are just that – specific to the emergency and likely to run off

anyhow as no longer needed, once recovery is secure. To be sure, the level of government debt will be higher, but the interest cost of this is orders of magnitude smaller than the extra debt in question.
- Especially in the context of a carbon tax being introduced, the fiscal stance of the public sector will have to accommodate the likely greater saving and certainly lesser investment needs of an ageing population, meaning private sector financial surpluses.

In a similar demographic context, Japan attempted to balance the budget in 2002–07, and again after the GFC with a 2014 consumption tax increase. But that led straight into renewed recession. For some years now Japan has simply accepted that never-ending budget deficits are the inevitable consequence of a large structural financial surplus in the private sector (i.e. a savings glut). The alternative to budget deficits as the counterpart to private financial surpluses is a current-account (trade) surplus with the rest of the world. That means exporting capital and deflating other countries. The counterpart to Japan's surpluses, which grew in 2002–07 alongside those of China and German-centred north-central Europe, was deficits and borrowing elsewhere in the world (US, UK/Ireland, Mediterranean Europe) leading to the US subprime debt crisis and GFC, plunging Japan (and the world) back into severe recession.

The key to dealing with rising government debt ratios and the ageing of populations has to be promotion of faster growth after the slippage of growth trends in recent decades. The world

Figure 20   Labour productivity since 1998 (7-year-moving-average % growth)

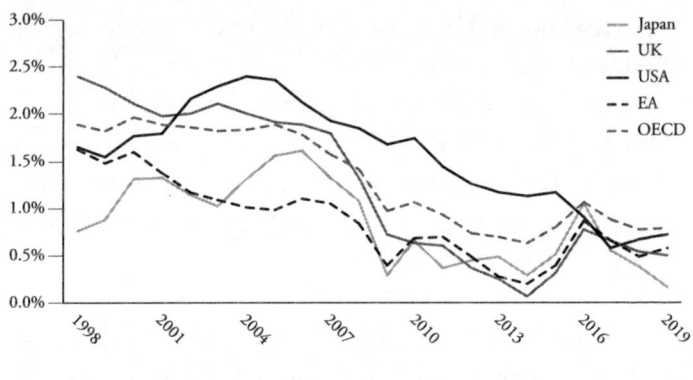

Sources: OECD, TS Lombard

will provide scope for that in the electrification of developing countries and other innovations needed to cope with climate change, as summarised in Essay 2. Both in the US and Europe inward-looking 'sound-money' people are discredited: in the US, Trump undermined his own Republican Tea Party people; in Europe the euro crisis saw excess-debt problems worsened, at best postponed while not improved, by austerity budgets.

Japan has slipped over thirty years into a pattern of slow growth and wasteful over-investment ('bridges to nowhere') funded by excessive domestic saving. But the US and UK economies have not slipped into the sluggish long-term growth path of Japan (and the Eurozone including Germany – see Figure 20 above). Running moderate deficits indefinitely does not necessitate a Japanese-style debt build-up, provided the economy is growing. And under-investment over the past twenty to thirty years should be corrected by essential decarbonisation and capex, both public and private.

Select bibliography to Essay 1

Dumas, C. E., 'US balance sheets serially trashed by Eurasian surplus', Lombard Street Research, *Monthly International Review*, No. 143, 2004

—*Globalisation Fractures: How Major Nations' Interests are Now in Conflict*, Profile Books, 2010

Keynes, J. M., *The General Theory of Employment, Interest and Money*, Macmillan, 1936

King, M. A., *The End of Alchemy: Money, Banking and the Future of the Global Economy*, W. W. Norton & Co., 2016

Wolf, M. H., *Why Globalization Works*, Yale University Press, 2004

Zucman, G., *The Hidden Wealth of Nations: The Scourge of Tax Havens*, University of Chicago Press, 2015

Essay 2

Climate change

Introduction

Climate change has been a big public issue for more than thirty years. This author has analysed and forecast the world economy since before the turn of the century. Yet those analyses and forecasts have been largely unaffected by climate change and the debate about it. G7 meetings have concluded each year with no more than a bow in the direction of combating climate change, and at G20 meetings, which include many developing nations that reject responsibility for climate change, it is even less of a priority. In the twenty years to 2019 the world's rate of carbon dioxide (CO_2) emission increased by 48 per cent, nearly a half. The explosion on to the world economic scene of China was the chief reason; its CO_2 emissions rose nearly three times in those twenty years, and are now 29 per cent of the world total. India's emissions growth was close to China's, despite slower, though still very rapid, economic growth. But both these Asian giants depend heavily on coal, and it is the downswing of cost of renewables-sourced electricity that holds out the chance of effective combat against climate change before it provokes disaster.

What else has changed to justify this book? Four things. First and foremost, the advanced-economy pressure to develop renewable sources of energy has led to scale economies in solar and wind technology that have made combating climate change a potential net plus for human welfare, particularly favouring the global south, especially low-income countries in Africa and Latin America – meanwhile rendering fossil-fuelled electricity generation potentially obsolescent. Second, policies to combat climate change are now being introduced on a fuller scale in many countries and should have big effects on incomes, spending and welfare as conventionally understood (and measured). Third, international businesses are increasingly taking account of climate change, especially decarbonisation, in their allocation of capital, with big effects on economic potential. Lastly, climate change and policies concerning it will generate big losers – and big winners. Discussion of climate change can now be about profit, no longer just the threat of disaster whose gloomy ring may have contributed to the weak global response so far to the issue.

This book, about the emergence of climate change as a major factor in how the world economy, population and politics develop, starts from the aftermath and effects of Covid-19, which not only provoked in 2020 the most severe global recession since the Black Death of 1348 (in Europe at least, including wartimes; what was happening at the time in America is unclear, and Asia also had plagues during this period too), it also changed the spending habits and general behaviour of people in the world's advanced economies. And just before Covid-19 came along, the world saw the fracturing of 1991–2016's globalisation by the end of America's benign neglect of China's explosion on to the world economy. There is now a full-scale struggle for economic and political primacy between the US and China, a struggle that is likely to be with us, unresolved, for the foreseeable future. This struggle has been aggravated by Covid-19, which originated in China and has added in various ways to the fracturing of globalisation.

This book is not a primer on climate change, least of all the physics, for which we are obliged to accept the overwhelming consensus of the relevant scientists – that it is man-made. It makes heavy use of the work of others, while focusing not so much on what should be done – what policies *should* be adopted – but rather on *what is actually likely to happen*, what policies are actually likely to be adopted. In analysing what needs to be done about climate change, the chief guide is Bill Gates' early-2021 book, *How to Avoid a Climate Disaster*.

Gates' book is an excellent hands-on guide to what can be done within existing technology, and what tech changes and inventive developments are needed to cope with climate change between now and the (intended and hoped-for) achievement of net-zero emissions in 2050. He is positive, knowledgeable, realistic and not at all puritanical, a relief from the hair-shirt doomsters that proliferate in climate-change commentary, though to be fair to, for example, the Stern report of late 2006 (a major analysis of the economics of climate change – see below) Gates' 'can-do' approach is made much more possible by plunging renewables-sourced electricity costs. But when it comes to the policies needed to achieve the needed changes, Gates' book is weak.

This weakness appears to arise because Gates' focus seems to be on restoring what might be called the 'American way of life' while minimising climate change – in other words, he pulls his punches. The chief proposal of this book is utterly conventional for an economist, namely the global adoption of carbon accounting and, based on that, a carbon tax. Such a tax, or some other method of putting a price on carbon emissions, is almost certainly essential to motivate decarbonisation. As a correspondent recently put it, climate change is the 'mother of all externalities', and the economics of externalities is well understood: government should tax the 'bad' and subsidise the 'good'. Among other points, the risk that rogue operators, in the face of official commitments to net zero, may try to preserve fossil-fuel activities at a lower level of prices would be reduced by an effective carbon tax that rendered such activities unprofitable.

Climate change is radically altering the style of economic development and growth. For the past 250 years, a quarter-millennium, the resources of the earth have been exploited by humans with increasing effect. Various inventions have contributed to this: coal-based steam power and simple heat, then electricity, more recently energy from gas and oil, and lastly electronic and tech developments that depend heavily on electricity. Harnessing such energy resources, transport and communication have been transformed from horseback to railways and then telephones, through cars, trucks and then aeroplanes to the contemporary profusion of tech. All this has supported rising standards of living – though largely concentrated in the minority of humanity that originated this industrial, and now service, revolution: the 'advanced' countries which now enjoy mass welfare. The distribution of income and wealth, rather than its generation, is raising increasingly tough policy issues quite apart from the question of how to combat climate change.

Thirty years of worry about climate change is a short time in an earth-science context – typical eras last thousands of years. Now, suddenly (in the earth-science sense) we have the threat of negative feedback from the earth itself. The whole form of human dominance of nature is questioned. Global atmospheric warming is not only disturbing weather patterns, species locations and agricultural potential – mostly with destructive effect, initially at least – it is also gradually warming the oceans that cover more than 70 per cent of the earth's surface, leading to hurricanes, rising sea level, and the disturbance of marine life, which is often more intertwined with human welfare than is understood, let alone acknowledged. This is not familiar to traditional governance and policymaking. Even the organisation of the world into nation states makes us less well equipped to deal with it. Likewise, economic theory, though the theory of public goods is a start.

We are mostly familiar with the concept of externalities. At a mundane level, this can simply mean that a privately optimal decision like commuting by car can, if done by the bulk of people, impose unacceptable economic costs (in this case, congestion, or maybe air pollution), so we tax cars and subsidise public transport, like trains and buses. But such a policy depends on broad public acceptance of the externality in question. This may be quite easily achieved on major moral questions; murder in pursuit of economic gain, for example, is clearly wrong and illegal. Cure for an externality can be achieved with persuasion where a particular problem becomes prominent, e.g. air pollution, but the acceptance of climate change as a dangerous form of air pollution has proved controversial, both in rich countries and rapidly developing poorer countries (or emerging markets – EMs).

All this is transformed by the newly competitive cost structure of wind and solar power, the key renewables as energy sources. The problem ceases to be one of persuasion – least of all that a scientific theory like climate change can be proved (not least because *no* scientific theory can be proved) – but becomes instead a problem of stranded assets, the new phrase for obsolescence. Who are the winners, and who are the losers from the transformation of relative energy costs? The answer is largely political, as it is with the question of how to combat climate change. Not the smallest of the issues is that cheap power from the wind and sun radically favours the global south, notably Africa and South America, and is least favourable to advanced economies with large, developed fossil-fuelled power systems, notably northern Europe and the Pacific rim (Japan, the Koreas and Taiwan) but also to a lesser extent North America. Who will handle obsolescence well, and who will handle it badly?

How quickly will the climate change? Perceptions vary, even within the consensus among scientists that man made climate change is happening, and increasing public acceptance of the need for action – spurred in many cases by extreme-weather events and the recent news that global warming has already exceeded 1°, and may reach 1½° by 2025. Does this affect the scale of response needed? Arguably not. We do not have the luxury of waiting to find out which of the options is correct: mild, serious or catastrophic damage. If the pace of change turns out to be slow and mild, and we have adopted measures that assume catastrophe, it would be a simple matter to apply such measures more gently, perhaps not at all. But if climate change is so rapid as to threaten catastrophe, the adoption of only modest measures to deal with it will quickly lead to crisis – followed in the traditional way by a draconian dose of too much, too late. In fact, without it being explicitly chosen, this is quite likely anyhow.

There are too many obstacles, mostly political, to the likely emergence of Gates' 'rosy scenario'. The politics and policies around climate change are too thorny for easy treatment, and much too thorny for the often idealistic recommendations of many green analyses and proposals, such as the recent programme from the International Energy Agency (IEA) to restrain global warming to 1½° by 2050.

Figure 21 (opposite, from the Stern report on climate change, 2006) shows 90 per cent confidence ranges around his forecasts. But it contains an implicit disaster zone, which is an outcome more than 35 per cent down from the business-as-usual (BAU) expectation over the two-centuries-long term for which he provides projections. But there are a variety of parts to the argument that will be politically important if measures to combat climate change are to be accepted.

The first point to deal with is the whole issue of the long-run trend. In the Stern report, the BAU baseline was 2 per cent annual growth of gross world product of which 1.3 per cent

Figure 21 **Why should we combat climate change now?**
% of gross world product

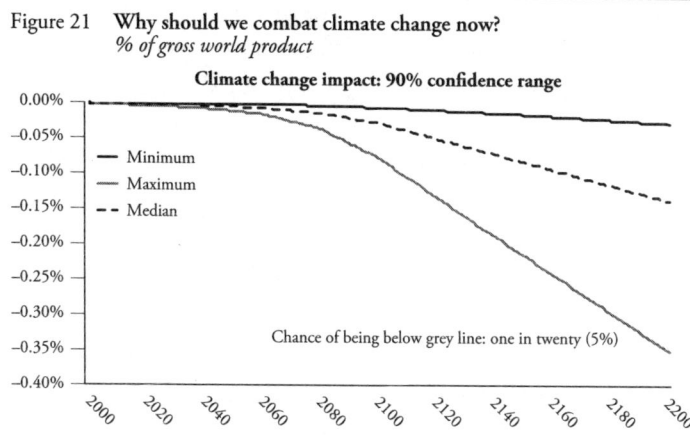

was projected to be real growth per capita. But climate-change sceptics, and others arguing against the need for strong policies, quite reasonably point out that 1.3 per cent annual growth would increase 2200's real GWP per head to 13¼ times 2000's. So the light grey line in Figure 21 (bottom of the 90 per cent confidence range) still leaves 2200 real incomes as much as 8.6 times 2000's and no doubt less unequally distributed than now. (LDCs will grow most). Why should this be regarded as a problem?

A feature of the Stern report is that it does not allow for any climate-change effects on the world's total population, e.g. famine or simply less food production with voluntary restraint of reproduction (or enforced restraint, as for several decades after 1979 in China). A recent question posed in London's Political Economy Club's bicentenary essay competition was 'With

UK real income per head up 15 times over the past 200 years and more evenly distributed, will this be repeated over the next 200 years? – and if not, why not?' The multiple of 15 times over 200 years was not a stretch, requiring 1.36 per cent annual growth, similar to Stern's projection. In the context of well-publicised risks to food supplies from climate change, a radical answer to the essay question for the whole world might be 'Yes' – but with real product/incomes unchanged over two centuries, and the world population shrunk by 15 times from a little over 7½ billion now to 500 million. That scenario would yield a very different aggregate real-income growth rate from the Stern report's, i.e. zero rather than 2 per cent a year, but per head it would still be 15 times today's.

This raises one of the major snags in plans to combat climate change: neither China nor India nor other EM countries have been prepared to accept penalties to combat climate change where the result might be slower catch-up growth vis-à-vis the West. (This catch-up was the chief source of world economic growth in 1990–2020.) Their point is a strong one. Whereas it is perfectly legitimate for the West to have pursued income-expanding policies over the past 250 years in the form of the Industrial Revolution and its successors, the likely global warming that is the result of these policies will harm everyone – but especially the left-behind EMs. In effect, the EM argument is: 'The West caused it, so the West can pay to cure it – and pronto, please, as it is harming us, even though we have not had nearly as large a benefit yet from the Industrial Revolution.'

Aside from this dictum being unenforceable, its weaknesses include the fact that the EMs depend on the West on a day-to-day basis for trade (and in a myriad of other ways) without which they will not catch up anyhow. But the emergence of China as an economy comparable to North America and Europe has shifted the balance of power decisively in favour of LDCs, whose economies now make up nearly 60 per cent of the world total, a ratio that increases every year. India's potential growth is now faster than China's, which could well now be 'down' to 5 per cent a year, compared with about 2 per cent in America, with Western Europe and Japan's annual growth at 1 per cent or less. As India's economy becomes comparable in size with China's, the power of LDCs will grow further. But their resistance to combating climate change is weakening, not least as poorer countries may suffer the most from it. Importantly as well, the carbon-tracker study used to show the fast-falling cost of renewables-generated electricity (wind power and solar panels) suggests superior ratios of solar capacity to land-area-plus-current-electricity-usage favours Africa and Latin America, especially vis-à-vis Japan and northern Europe, though the study concludes that US, China and India are fully viable vis-à-vis solar and wind power.

The world's population growth is in any case slowing down, though there is no shrinkage yet. Its annual growth rate peaked at about 2 per cent around 1950 and remains over 1 per cent. But current projections have the global population rising from 7.8 billion now to nearly 11 billion by 2100, by when its growth rate is forecast (by the UN) to be minimal, little over 0.1 per cent a year – though 0.1 per cent of 11 billion people is still 11 million people. Shrinkage is occurring already in Europe and Pacific-rim countries, and is expected soon in China. The growth projected is in south Asia, south-east Asia, Africa and Latin America, with continued growth likely in North America. These population forecasts over the balance of the twenty-first century are in any case improbable. As LDCs catch up with Western prosperity, the need for children – in many cultures the chief source of old-age care – could shrink rapidly as infant healthcare improves. And greater prosperity also tends to cut family size. Measures to combat climate change could accelerate that.

Rapid population growth is, indeed, one thing humanity has to fear in all the apocalyptic talk about human extinction. To talk of the threat to the planet (as people do) is wide of the mark. The planet will survive and continue to revolve round the sun (as it always has) under any scenario for humanity. The climate-change threat is to the human race plus many other species besides ourselves. This book will only deal tangentially with the theory of James Lovelock that the earth – Gaia in his usage – is a live entity that will evolve via a benign sloughing-off of the human race. But it is important to note the recent point of the Intergovernmental Panel on Climate Change (IPCC) that 'Life on earth can recover from major climate change by evolving new species and creating new ecosystems ... but humanity cannot recover.' The assumption here is that by some means, however desperate, humanity will do whatever it takes to survive.

'Whatever it takes' may not be much fun. A darker, perhaps more realistic, potential political scenario is that combined complacency and obstinacy prevent, or slow to a crawl, the development of the measures Gates and environmentalists correctly regard as urgent. It seems entirely possible that only some malignant result of climate change – such as desertification, famine, rising sea level or major hurricanes – finally tips the world into correction mode, in other words doing too much, too late. The possibilities to be examined (see pages 105–07) are those outlined by Mark Lynas in his 2007 *Six Degrees*, a seven-chapter book with the first six chapters looking at likely consequences of global warming by 1°, 2°, 3°, etc. As 3° of total global warming is a likely maximum before calamity provokes emergency action, the list of possible downsides that might provoke such action will exclude the gruesome scenarios in the latter half of his book (i.e. Chapters 4–6 covering warming of 4°–6°).

Three degrees is in any case the scale of global warming likely within this century with the current, half-hearted policy approach. The International Energy Agency in Paris recently came out with its own report on net-zero greenhouse gases (GHGs) by 2050, which was the goal set in the Paris IPCC accord of 2015 intended to limit global warming to 1.5° by mid-century. But a too much, too late war on climate change could make the restraints on human freedom we have endured in the Covid-19 crisis seem like a picnic in the park. Interestingly, the much more politically stratified Asian and Pacific-rim countries brought Covid-19 under control much faster than the West, though Covid-19 has proved able to serve up a few unpleasant surprises. Sadly, the IEA report's weaknesses may make it as futile as previous cries in the dark about climate change over the past thirty years or more. Specifically, the IEA report said that fulfilment of net-zero pledges that have so far been made (mostly by advanced economies) would lead to 2050 global temperatures being 2.1°, not 1½°, higher.

There are at least two major reasons why the IEA's report may fail to achieve its goals. The first is that developed-economy countries may pull their punches in implementing measures the IEA recommends (see page 77, with itemisation on pages 105–07). The second is that some countries may decide to play dirty vis-à-vis these measures. Suppose, for example, that a major member of OPEC decides to cut a side deal with a major oil/gas importer at a low oil price that nonetheless covers the (very low) cost of oil extraction in the Middle East. Or perhaps Russia, not enjoying energy extraction costs as low as e.g. Saudi Arabia, may get itself into an economic tangle and take the short-term step of pumping fossil fuels out into the world.

Freedom-loving people in the West have had, of course, a foretaste of life under curtailed liberties since March 2020. So understanding the issues raised by Covid-19 and the resulting violent recession, important anyhow, also anticipates what may be necessary if the world does not measure up adequately to the climate-change challenge.

Writing about combating climate change for an economist is made difficult by the implications of the growth of real income per head. In the perspective of traditional economics, consideration of human welfare has not hitherto taken account of biodiversity (e.g. the extermination of other species resulting from humans striving for their own welfare). But such anthropocentrism, given the present pace of global warming and climate change, can be challenged not only for its morality but also for its practical risks, given the radical threat of climate change to human welfare itself. The utilitarian process of economic reasoning is purely anthropocentric, arguably alienated from nature, which mankind manipulates to its advantage. Economists are not in their professional capacity required to consider anything beyond the consequences of changes for the welfare of humanity, of human beings and human society, with due consideration of the distribution of income, for example, but without regard for the animal kingdom, let alone vegetables and marine life. Much of the ecological case for action against climate change is based on such issues as the extinction of species by climate change. For example, the preservation of coral reefs, which feature in much commentary on climate change, is beyond economic analysis as well as being insignificant for global economic growth. While there have been recent attempts to measure the economic value of nature, the results fall well short of being tried and tested.

With global warming, the ideal northern-hemisphere location for numerous species will gradually move north – and south in the southern hemisphere. But the adaptation of species to their optimal living conditions moving north may be prevented, even where it is physically feasible, by the speed of climate change or by man-made obstructions to species movement. This is beyond the scope of economic analysis. But what economics can do is identify the risks in one scenario versus another. So for this purpose in this book, two scenarios will be:

A. Measures to achieve net-zero carbon emissions by mid-century (2050 in advanced countries, 2060 or later in LDCs) followed by the continued progress of such measures so that human economic activity is net negative in carbon emissions well before the end of the twenty-first century – the policy recommended here.

B. Acceptance of the global warming resulting from business as usual with global carbon emissions lessened over time by the obsolescence of fossil-fuelled electricity generation, and awareness that huge adaptations to climate change will probably be needed – not least because of rising sea level – quite possibly in the second half of this century though in the twenty-second century for sure, by when (on reasonable projections) human welfare will be multiples of current levels, permitting the relative cost of adaptation to be less.

The choice between A and B is not purely economic. But several important points can be made.

- The discount rate to be applied to future welfare is a key factor. On the (normal) assumption that per capita real income will grow, a larger discount rate would bias the argument in favour of A, as the importance of real-income growth, the chief reason for preferring B, is reduced. Likewise, a low discount rate, especially as regards the 'pure time-value of money' factor in the analysis below, favours B.
- Scenario B is not unlike the world policies of the past thirty to forty years that have enabled absolute poverty to be dramatically reduced and the shift in world income in favour of LDCs to develop. Since 1990, however, world atmospheric concentrations of GHGs are up by nearly half. B would be favoured if the effects of carbon emissions on the world's temperature turn out to be less than currently forecast. B is the high-risk scenario, but it would not avoid the cumulative effects, many of them felt over centuries or even millennia, of

accepting the rise in temperature from atmospheric carbon that has already been emitted, with emissions intensifying further under B.

- B involves the near certainty that the sea level will rise substantially. The last time the atmospheric concentration of carbon was at current levels (let alone those likely by 2100 under B) the sea level was some twenty-five metres (eighty feet) higher than now. This would pose a major threat to, for example, Florida and Houston, much of London and New York, Ho Chi Minh City and the Mekong delta, Shanghai, Kolkata and the whole of Holland and Bangladesh – to name just some obvious places.
- While humanity could adapt to such land loss, especially if the world population shrinks, the risks in scenario B are large. The development of human civilisation has occurred in the Holocene climatic era of the past 10,000 years, since the last ice age, with essentially the current sea level and temperature. For the animal and vegetable kingdom we are used to (and have modified to meet human needs) the effects of substantial and sustained global warming are way into the realm of the unknown, as they are for both sea temperatures and marine life.

Ultimately, this last point amounts to the moral question of whether human domination of the earth gives us guardianship responsibility for the whole of nature. The case cannot be proven either way in economic terms. In this book the assumed goal is therefore scenario A above, with one important proviso: if the meteorological science remains much as understood now, and as assumed in the analysis of the IPCC, the move to net-zero GHG emissions will have to be followed by a continuation into net-negative GHGs. This is fundamental to policies that are (small c) conservative as regards the environment. The principle being followed here requires the unwinding of global warming by reduced atmospheric GHGs as soon as possible after the world reaches net zero.

Economics is essential to analysing the discount rate. Frank Ramsey in the 1920s at Cambridge was cited earlier in relation to the risk of slower long-term growth owing to a quasi-permanent global savings glut (page 3). A powerfully original mind, he also developed the equation or formula for defining the discount rate to be applied to the welfare consequences of policies. It is relevant to policies to combat climate change.

Whatever the leaning of an analyst concerning the trade-off between the welfare of future generations and the present population, the correct discount rate is defined in algebraic terms by Ramsey's equation, which says the discount rate should be the sum of the per capita real-income growth rate adjusted for the marginal social utility of extra consumption plus the pure time-value of money. The precise formula is $R = \eta^*\gamma + \delta$, where R is the correct discount rate to be applied to aggregate future welfare, η is the elasticity of the social marginal utility of consumption (neutrally taken by Stern to be 1), γ is the growth rate of real income per capita and δ is the pure time-value of money, all expressed at annual rates. Stern reaches his 1.4 per cent for R by taking the per capita growth rate as 1.3 per cent (in effect, his 2 per cent growth rate of the world's gross product minus population growth projected at 0.7 per cent a year in the twenty-first century), the marginal elasticity of consumption vis-à-vis real income gains to be 1, and a deliberately minimal time-value of 0.1 per cent to reflect the possibility of human extinction – taken as 10 per cent per century.

There is a cruel paradox at the heart of Stern's analysis. If the chances of human extinction are higher, use of the Ramsey formula would raise R and thus reduce the present value of future human welfare. This higher discount rate would weaken the argument for strong action against climate change as the present value of such strong action would be reduced.

For large numbers of the world population, the risk of their personal extinction by premature death is raised by prospective climate change, regardless of the fate of humanity as a whole. So Stern's provision of 0.1 per cent for extinction, a 10 per cent chance of extinction for each of the two centuries of his analysis, looks inadequate if climate change may kill large numbers – by famine, for example. Yet if his δ were raised, less would – or applying the Ramsey formula should – be done to offset one of the chief possible sources of, if not the extinction of the human race, at least millions of deaths through famine, flooding and desertification, as may result from climate change. In other words, accepting population projections as a given distorts the analysis of policy. An optimal policy to deal with negative potential effects of climate change has to work in a variety of possible population scenarios, and preferably involves at least the reduction of the growth of world population, ideally its actual decline over the long run.

However, there are good grounds for challenging all the elements of Stern's analysis. When it comes to the marginal utility of consumption, the number 1 seems on the high side. For Bill Gates, for example, the marginal utility of extra income is clearly zero – arguably, the *social* marginal utility is actually negative in his case, especially if his extra income arises through monopoly practices or perhaps gets spent on items that aggravate climate change (private plane flights, for example). But invidious finger-pointing weakens analysis of climate change.

This gets us back to the post-Covid situation in which people simply want to restore 'normality'. Thus this writer, born in 1946, took a ration book with him when he first went to school (1951) but for more than the past fifty years has been able, whenever he wants, to go into a pub and order a pint of beer. For more than a year he could not do that, and drinking beer at home is definitely not the same. As an Irish wit said early on in the Covid lockdowns, 'If they don't reopen the pubs soon, we'll all be alcoholics.' It can be argued that economically we had by 2019 already 'made it' in terms of ultimate living standards – in the West at least, including for this purpose Japan and other developed Asian/Australasian countries. Arguably, the marginal social utility of extra consumption in the West is not all that much above zero.

Of course, this approach downplays the effects of inequality in the West – which has mostly increased over the past thirty to forty years, especially if capital assets are taken into account – and the need for lower-income people to be better off. More importantly, the West in this sense only comprises about one billion people, so the other 6¾ billion people on earth are naturally keen to improve their standard of living to match the West's. But even for a poor peasant in a south Asian or African village, the marginal utility of extra income is likely to be less than that of the first dollar – a dollar that may have enabled starvation to be avoided. So on a worldwide basis an elasticity of 1 for social utility is almost certainly too high.

However, Stern may be a bit mean in saying growth per capita will only be 1.3 per cent. My former colleague Brian Reading looked at the whole twentieth century for a note in 2000 and came up with 1½ per cent as the per capita real-income growth rate over 100 years for both the US and the UK. World growth has been exceeding this so far this century as EMs gradually catch up. Taking this into account, the global product of the growth rate (higher than Stern's) and the true extra welfare it brings (lower) may well be guesstimated to be 1 per cent or so, compared to Stern's 1.3 per cent (decimal points implying greater precision than is justified by this analysis).

When it comes to the time-value of money, Stern's view is highly controversial and has been challenged by US economists such as William Nordhaus, whose analysis of climate change (among other things) earned him the Nobel Prize for Economics.

Before discussing this point, the issue of humanity's extinction merits a moment's side glance. Two recent books have addressed it: *Novacene* (2019) by James Lovelock (originator of the Gaia thesis – see page 76) and *The Precipice* (2020) by Toby Ord, an Oxford philosopher and philanthropist. In the latter, the chances of humanity's extinction by various means are assessed, concluding that extinction by climate change is unlikely. The chances of human survival from climate change are high on any reasonable reckoning, even if the resulting lifestyle of the survivors might be considered unacceptable to current citizens of the West.

The chief contrast between these two visions of the future lies in Lovelock's benign view of AI simply taking over the world. He believes in such a takeover, which he calls 'evolution', and appears to welcome it. Ord's point is that malignant AI might simply choose to destroy us. He identifies this as the chief risk of human extinction. Worth noting is that the word 'robot' was originated by the Czech writer Karel Čapek in a play written in 1920, the word derived from 'slave' in Slavic languages. The thought behind Ord's fear is that AI might develop a will of its own and reject its slavery by killing off the enslavers, i.e. us. Lovelock believes that robots would quickly use their superior brains to calculate that killing off humanity is not to their advantage. But of course we know from numerous examples that humans sometimes do not act in their own best interests, and AI and robots are a human invention/extension.

The key point from this diversion is that climate change is not so much an existential threat to humanity as a threat to a Panglossian Whig view of history, i.e. a smooth continuation of the progress achieved by humanity in the 250 years since the Industrial Revolution. That is the context in which we need to consider what discount should be applied to the future welfare of humanity in considering what resources to devote now to combat climate change.

Stern's wish to set the time-value of money essentially at zero places him in a long tradition of English philosophers (wrongly) called utilitarians, going back at least to Sidgwick in the nineteenth century. (Ramsey and Pigou in early-twentieth-century

Cambridge were part of this.) Their insight is that future generations are as important as ourselves – as Ramsey put it 'to suppose otherwise shows lack of imagination', showing an arrogance not unusual for a twenty-five-year-old genius.

Can fewer people be part of the solution?

The key point in this discussion is the possibility that the world in future might be a better place if its human population were much smaller. In that case, under any scenario for the appropriate discount rate applicable to future welfare, any sacrifice of current living standards needed to combat potential damage from climate change would be smaller. But such a conclusion only applies if the population shrinkage is part of an agreed process for tackling climate change involving most of the world's governments and people. The regrettable truth is that a future with far fewer humans is much more likely to arise through climate-change disasters like famine, desertification and floods than through concerted internationally agreed action. So Ramsey's phrase 'lack of imagination' clearly does not apply to this context – it is no aid to good analysis.

Apart from this interactive aspect of the analysis of the appropriate discount rate to apply to the welfare of future generations, there are three major reasons to be sceptical of the English utilitarian school's view that a zero discount rate should apply. In ascending order of importance these are:

1. Symmetry between the future and the past. Such symmetry may not be thought important, but it is reasonable to ask

whether (for example) the Duke of Wellington was thinking of my interests when he fought 1815's Battle of Waterloo, and indeed whether he should have been thinking of my interests. In case anyone jumps to a simple patriotic answer to this question, we can ask the same questions about Napoleon's invasion of Russia in 1812 and today's interests of the French. It is only too clear that the questions are close to ridiculous. And one of many reasons why those leaders did not have those questions foremost in their minds is that the future is highly uncertain. That high uncertainty in itself increases the appropriate discount rate applicable to some presumed level of human welfare.

2. The more we cut, the more we have to cut. The world population at the end of this century is generally expected to be larger than today's. But if sharp cuts in today's welfare were to increase both the 2100 population and its average welfare, then arguably we should cut even more, if that future welfare is not heavily discounted: cuts could become a net-positive-sum game. For example, if consumption cuts of 2 per cent now were to result in the 2320 population being 4 per cent higher without any loss of per capita income growth, the argument for greater sacrifices today would be overwhelming, and only subject to any limit if diminishing returns were to apply. As observed already, economic growth, at least in hourly productivity, is likely to continue for the foreseeable future to outweigh any sacrifices of welfare to combat climate change. In other words, future populations will be better off – their welfare is for them to attend to, as much as or more than for us today.

3. The fallacy of determinism. Werner Heisenberg's 1927 enunciation of his uncertainty principle means determinism as a principle, going back at least to Descartes and Spinoza in the seventeenth century, is utterly discredited. Heisenberg pointed out that to determine the position of an elementary particle one had to change its velocity, and to determine its velocity one has to change its position. So it is not possible to know its position and velocity at the same time. Without knowing that about elementary particles, determinism collapses. Radical uncertainty about the future cannot be avoided. To assess the future welfare effects of actions today is therefore impossible. The best we can do is to make forecasts based on the best available methods and information. The long-term economic forecasts needed to vindicate any given sacrifice of current welfare have little validity. One can forgive Ramsey, who was born in 1903, being unaware of Heisenberg's work, but it invalidates his views about the balance between current and future welfare.

Ramsey was an explicit socialist as well as a great mathematician, economist and philosopher, and 1920s Britain saw widespread misery as the government attempted to hold to the gold standard at the pre-World War I price. One result was the 1926 General Strike, as employers sought wage cuts. But that was then, and this is now. The socialism common in Cambridge between the wars is not a promising guide for today.

The phrase 'bawling on paper' was coined by Jeremy Bentham to describe the 1789 Declaration of the Rights of Man. Human rights, however, have been a useful political principle (if logically weak, which is Bentham's point). But a zero time-value of money looks both logically weak and useless – bawling on paper indeed. Its flavour of power-crazed puritanism should not be part of the climate-change debate. Generally, it is likely that puritanical alarmism has been a significant factor causing climate-change denial and the thirty years of inadequate response to it.

Before outlining the case for combating climate change, the last point (3) above refuting determinism might be thought to undermine the whole basis for such a case. But that would be to misunderstand the whole nature of science. It is banal to observe that there is no such thing as a scientific fact (though people often ask for exactly that). Scientific method is to test a theory by trying to disprove it. Until it is disproved, a theory remains tenable, and if confirmed by a lot of evidence may even be referred to as a 'law'. For example, it was to explain observed weaknesses in Newtonian mechanics – his laws of motion and gravity – that Einstein developed his Special and General relativity theories. Poincaré, the leading French physicist at the time, also came up with Special Relativity, but was trying to shore up Newtonian physics; Einstein's vision was that this could not be done. One paradox of climate change is that its occurrence is a consensus among the relevant scientists, yet it has not been – and cannot be – subject to standard disproof tests normal for scientific theories.

The problem with the theory of climate change is that the experiment that might disprove it – and would, as a result, vindicate it if it is correct – would involve doing nothing and seeing the results. Under the theory, this would be catastrophic.

Arguably, this has in fact been the course so far pursued by the governments of the world with a few honourable exceptions, though in their defence must be cited the progress in renewables electricity – assuming that we now use that progress to avoid the worst risks of damage.

As it happens, the pace of climate change, especially in polar ice-melt but also extreme weather, is proceeding with greater virulence than the consensus of relevant scientists has predicted (perhaps their predictions were downplayed in a concession to climate-change sceptics, of whom there have been, and still are, many). The science in question has, by its very nature, *not* been testable (or tested) by the principal scientific method: running experiments to disprove it. Such experiments would require exposing people to huge risks in 'counterfactual' developments. But the combination of the consensus of relevant scientists with the success of the forecasts so far amounts to a persuasive case for action.

What sort of action? It is tempting to frame the argument for measures to combat climate change as if they were a form of insurance. This approach is intuitively attractive but wrong. With house insurance, for example, or most other forms of insurance, when/if disaster strikes you can simply use the insurance money to mend the damage or buy another house. Combating climate change is akin to national defence: we do not know what threats we may face, but we have to make the best estimates we can, and in general provide for the worst. So this book deals with the economics of avoiding catastrophe and, where possible, profiting from climate change and decarbonisation. Clearly, the search for profit could not be at this stage the motivation for assuming the reasonable worst case. But that simply reflects the obvious point that the lead will have to come from public policy to deal with this 'mother of all externalities'. Interestingly, business circles are increasingly critical on exactly this point: the lack of a coherent public policy framework.

Carbon taxes are essential

What did Big Tobacco do when the medics proved that smoking damages health in multiple ways, not just lung cancer? It tried to trash the science and spent money lobbying heavily. What does Big Oil (and Big Coal and Big Gas) do when faced with the scientific consensus on climate change? It tries to trash the science and slow down any combat against climate change by appealing to the unpopularity of measures that at the least disturb huge amounts of current habitual activities and probably mean significant cuts, at least for the time being, in people's standard of living. Fossil fuels may not be addictive drugs like tobacco, but they are not far short of that, having become fundamental to people's homes and their mobility.

Net-zero carbon emissions will not be achieved in any country by simply boosting budget spending. Billionaires have homes in many countries; given their addiction to travel, they may add to the weight of money fighting curbs on carbon emissions. But probably more important will be the weight of votes. It is not just billionaires that like to go on holiday, as we are finding out in the Covid crisis.

The example of Britain's Clean Air Act of 1956 shows democratic politics in action. Decades of London's killer 'pea-soupers' (smog-based dense fogs caused by burning coal as fuel) were allowed to continue as governments tried to blame them on business usage. But the true source of the smogs was the household hearths in which coal was the chief fuel. After some gruesome pea-soupers in the early-1950s recovery from World War II, the nettle was finally grasped, though one wonders how long that would have taken had it not been for town gas (mostly methane-based) and later natural gas from the North Sea (also methane-based). Electricity ('clean simplicity' went the advertising jingle – emphasis on the 'clean') was never competitively priced for the mass market – a point that electric-vehicle advocates may yet find working against overly simplistic climate-change measures favouring electric vehicles.

The only way to curb carbon emissions is to make emitting carbon an expensive option. That means a carbon tax, not emissions-trading systems (so-called cap and trade). Appendix 1 lists the various sources of GHG emissions. It is a shortened outline of climate-change effects from Bill Gates' book *How to Avoid a Climate Disaster* and it goes through the GHG sources item by item, starting with electric power generation, since the radical potential of low-cost renewables to make possible net zero by 2050 lies in switching to electric power where possible, rather than continued direct application of fossil fuels, mostly coal, gas and oil. It goes on to cover industry (globally the largest source of GHG emissions), transport, agriculture and premises (heating, lighting and air conditioning), reflecting the order of their respective contribution to GHG emissions.

The Gates book is an excellent primer as to what needs to be done – much less good on how to make sure it *is* done. The chief reason for this latter weakness is his unwillingness to state the obvious: only by putting a price on GHG emissions, penalising those that continue and rewarding both cuts in emissions and innovations that lead to such cuts, is it at all likely that the needed changes and innovations to get to net zero will occur.

Urging virtuous behaviour will certainly not be enough. For example, the IEA report on how to limit global warming to 1½°, that came out in May 2021 said all new fossil-fuel electricity generation should be stopped immediately. That was on a Tuesday (18 May). On Friday of that week, the G7 (major advanced economies) announced that all new coal-fuelled generation would be stopped – leaving open the use of gas, a lesser GHG-emitting fossil fuel that has been posited by industry apologists as crucial to the transition to renewables from coal. So the G7 was simply promising to do the easy bit – the bit they intended to do anyhow in transition to net zero. And even if the G7 and other countries that have promised net-zero GHGs by 2050 achieve this goal, the IEA analysis said that global warming would only be limited to 2.1°, not the IEA/IPCC's goal of 1½° – the reason being that the bulk of GHG emissions now occur in countries like China which are not committed to the 2050 net-zero date (2060 in China's case); for many others no net-zero commitment has been made.

Why should we adopt a carbon tax rather than extend the EU's cap and trade system?

The advantages of cap and trade schemes for carbon emissions are that they are relatively easy to administer and set some sort of price for carbon emissions. But the drawbacks are large: pure reliance on cap and trade, supplemented by official decarbonisation subsidies, is almost certainly too slow. Specifically, after recent decades of substantial progress in cutting advanced-countries' carbon emissions, CO_2 emissions are still increasing worldwide, raising the likely peak for global average temperature to late this century, by when the world will have had to become carbon negative, going well beyond the current goal of net zero by 2050. Yet the damaging effects of climate change are already evident, both in general weather patterns and the disappearance of the year-round Arctic ice cap. If GHG emissions are not reduced as a matter of urgency, the long-term damage, which derives from the *stock* of GHGs in the atmosphere not the net *flow* of new emissions, will be getting greater well into the twenty-second century. As I have noted, the last time atmospheric GHG concentrations were at current levels, the sea level was some twenty-five metres higher.

The flaws of reliance on cap and trade are clear.

- It really only works for reducing CO_2 emissions by major power suppliers – i.e. the possibility of cutting emissions embodied in imports does not arise, though it is to be attempted by the EU. Nor does it affect the major emissions of non-CO_2 carbon, even potent GHGs such as methane, including the delicate subject of farm animals' 'wind'.
- The caps are doled out *gratis* to existing energy suppliers, i.e. powerful lobbies, and are not tapered in line with an aggressive enough plan for reduced CO_2 emissions. This is a natural result of the low priority that has been given to combating climate change versus more mundane and conventional human welfare issues, as well as the effects of

established industries' lobbying. And there is the free-rider problem whereby higher energy costs put a country at a cost-competitive disadvantage.
- As with carbon taxes, which raise revenue, cap and trade creates winners and losers, but the latter are unknown entrepreneurs and the former closely linked to the current establishment. Winners and losers created thus may be 'politics as usual', but it is bad economics and unlikely to solve the problem posed by climate change. Only with a carbon tax will the hidden hand be truly hidden and do its work properly.
- Perhaps the most important downside of cap and trade is that it encourages the export of emissions-creating activities – chiefly heavy industries – to EMs like China and India, who then export the carbon-intensive products, e.g. cement, steel and plastics, back to the advanced economy that is employing cap and trade to reduce its own emissions. The EU rightly plans a border adjustment mechanism to offset this.
- In terms of responses by businesses to the steps needed to get to net zero, the price of a ton of carbon under cap and trade can and does fluctuate significantly, whereas a given rate of carbon tax would reduce the uncertainty inherent to the calculations of the relevant businesses.

Needless to say, carbon taxes have their drawbacks too, but they do create clear incentives to decarbonisation. The most obvious drawback – apart from offsettable downsides like the regressiveness of the tax – is administrative. A trickier long-run difficulty concerns current free-trade rules.

At this point, knowledge is limited on how much carbon is emitted into the atmosphere to create a ton of steel imported from China, let alone, to take a random example, to enable the widespread use of Microsoft Windows, though Microsoft has done a good job in its carbon accounting. Carbon accounting is essential, but in its infancy.

A carbon tax is therefore a ten-year project, first of all requiring the imposition on businesses of carbon accounting analogous to current financial accounting requirements. But it needs to be pushed forward as a matter of urgency. Such a tax applied across the board is the single strongest motivation a government can introduce for private-sector decarbonisation and the innovations described as essential in Appendix 1 (e.g. for carbon capture and storage).

On the free-trade point, an obstacle to a proper carbon tax is that levying it on imports will breach the treaties supporting the World Trade Organisation (formerly the General Agreement on Tariffs and Trade, GATT). So a proper carbon tax will involve first a major push to reform WTO rules. Sadly reflecting this, Biden's climate-change envoy John Kerry told the EU he regarded its approximation of a carbon levy on imports – its border adjustment mechanism – as a last resort. This anti-green observation is precisely the reverse of what is needed; the EU initiative, which should in any case be a first resort, is a big step in the right direction. The alternative to such a process for charging taxes on imported items like steel is, for example, punitive tariffs on items with heavy carbon content offset by provisions to exempt imports from such tariffs if their carbon content is fully accounted for and made liable to the carbon tax.

A difficult interim measure should be steps to discourage imports of goods and services with high carbon content. Foreign-country exporters that engage in full carbon accounting to demonstrate low carbon content should be exempted from the needed schedule of *presumed* carbon content that will certainly be needed for certain categories of imports. If such measures are rejected on the grounds that they challenge free trade, the world will in effect be condemned to a race to the bottom in permitting free-riders to acquire competitive cost advantage from fossil-fuel energy, which will be rendered cheaper by the needed measures to combat climate change (and possibly, as already mentioned, by malignant resistance to measures to achieve net zero).

In the interim needed to plan and implement carbon taxes, proxies for carbon taxes will be needed. These should include steps to shift the emphasis in decarbonisation policies towards ensuring that household energy usage is transformed, including, to take a UK example, raising the VAT rate on energy utilities to the standard 20 per cent rate, with the needed associated increases in social welfare, including old-age pensions, for poorer households. A similar fallacy vis-à-vis household energy use, as described on page 93 in connection with the UK's 1956 Clean Air Act, is excessive focus on carbon emissions by cars and especially aircraft, versus industrial and household use of fossil-fuel energy.

Taking advantage of the existing infrastructure for delivering gas to homes and elsewhere suggests vigorous investigation of the potential for hydrogen as fuel; it can serve the same purpose for cars and heavier vehicles like trucks. It is risky to rely purely on electrically driven vehicles or any other single approach that could prove vulnerable, unpredictability of events being one major lesson from Covid-19.

This illustrates one important idea behind a carbon tax: the classic search for tax neutrality. 'Sin taxes' on tobacco and alcohol originate in puritanical penal ideas, though tobacco taxes clearly raise revenue that helps pay for expensive health services to deal with the damage to health from smoking. This rationale, which also applies to some extent to alcohol taxes, clearly only applies to motoring taxes in relation to the specific social costs of motoring: the wear and tear on public roads, the noise and pollution from traffic, etc. The carbon tax idea is to ensure all forms of carbon emission are discouraged, the point being that emissions in (e.g.) China to make steel that is then exported elsewhere will affect the whole world's climate, not just China's. This justifies the growing focus on life-cycle analysis of GHG emissions. Measures to combat climate change must be closely examined to ensure they are *not* partial, e.g. only affecting transport. A carbon tax passes this test.

Carbon tax as an opportunity for the UK

It is tempting to see a carbon tax as an opportunity for a medium-sized economy with a well-developed financial sector, like the UK. The chief point is that most views about combating climate change focus on government expenditure, or at least regulation. This may well be needed, but the point of a carbon tax is that it could massively motivate decarbonisation while *raising revenue*. Here the analogy is with tobacco and alcohol taxes – and for puritans the virtue signal is that these are commonly called sin taxes. The heavy reliance of tax revenue on motoring taxes – both on petrol itself and car licences – is an extension of the sin-tax idea, the thought being that motoring is a luxury, as it indeed was in the old days.

A carbon tax at the level needed to achieve decarbonisation is widely thought to be in the $75–100/ton region. In the UK net carbon emissions are about 6½ tons per head per year. But the carbon content of UK economic activity, taking this to be close to the UK share of the world's GDP at comparable prices (so-called purchasing-power parity, or PPP), is about twice that. At $75–100/ton, a UK carbon tax could raise close to £70–90 billion. This is close to the current yield of corporation tax, whose abolition would both rationalise the taxation of business and draw large numbers of corporate HQs to the UK, with major revenue benefits. Clearly, the substitution of carbon tax for corporation tax would hurt poorer households, requiring compensating expenditure. But compared to spending on essentially speculative government schemes to combat climate change, carbon tax is certain to discourage carbon emissions, while the spending to support poorer households would demonstrate the clearly positive intentions of the tax. Some degree of gradualism is inevitable, but it is important to keep it to the minimum. And the offset from the inflow of company HQs could be significant.

The chief downside of this type of scheme is that its advantages partly arise from drawbacks for other countries at a time when the new US government under Biden is attempting to pull the world away from low-tax competition. In that sense, it would be similar to the tax dodges promoted by Ireland, Luxembourg and the Netherlands, for example, as well as the more extreme tax havens. For a trading nation such as the UK, this is a serious downside, but not one that argues against a carbon tax, and abolition of corporation tax is just one of many possible uses of the revenue. Moreover, the argument for carbon taxes is so strong – and potentially positive for Biden in pursuit of his high-spending US federal government programmes – that the new US acceptance of the need to minimise climate change should mitigate US official hostility. In this sense, the UK would simply be going down a similar – and similarly desirable – road to the EU, which is continuing its pursuit of what is tantamount to border levies on the carbon content of imports.

The biggest hurdle to get over with a carbon tax is the general point that it needs to be levied on imports to the extent that they embody carbon emissions. This raises the whole question of international cooperation in connection with combating climate change. The UK should in effect use a carbon tax plan, and the abolition of corporate income tax, as a lever to fight tax avoidance ploys in other countries. The hold that Ireland, Luxembourg and the Netherlands have over EU policies should prove a minor obstacle, given German enthusiasm for the border levy, especially in the light of German tax-revenue losses to the low-tax regimes of those three countries and the transition from a Luxembourgeois EU president (Juncker) to a German national (von der Leyen).

Nationalism in the context of combating climate change

The observation that nationalism is a threat to climate-change combat is both trivial in that it is obvious and at the same time profoundly important. While all may agree that carbon emissions anywhere can aggravate climate change – and it must be remembered that not everyone does agree on this – every country has its reasons why someone else should do the heavy lifting. Americans can complain that, as the leading big-country emitter per head of population, measures to cut emissions will have the biggest impact on them – and anyhow, it is not just a matter of cutting emissions, but also reabsorbing carbon through forestry, etc. where the US has a good track record. Meanwhile, China and India have until recently led the LDC charge that they should not have to sacrifice their catch-up with advanced countries because of the latter's long-term emissions record over the past quarter-millennium. These are all good points, but the worldwide benefit – necessity – of action is unaffected. It remains to be seen whether the competition to develop the technologies to combat climate change will take on a nationalistic tinge, which is not a bad thing if it spurs greater urgency.

Easily the biggest nationalistic threat to measures against climate change is Russia. It is relatively easy to dismiss the threat of a major Middle Eastern oil producer, Saudi Arabia for example, cutting a deal to sell oil at a major discount to recent price levels. Saudi policy is formed very much on the hoof so this process would only be gradual, spread over years in response to the emergence of oil's obsolescence and the consequent threat to revenues it has come to depend on. And of the major Middle Eastern oil exporters, only Saudi could contemplate the political consequences of such a ploy. Iran would risk revolution by such price cutting (though price cuts may undermine the present regime anyhow); Iraq among the major Middle Eastern oil exporters is too chaotic to implement such a policy effectively, and the rest (Kuwait, UAE and Bahrain) too small. Even a Saudi-led campaign for the whole of OPEC to cut prices in a reverse of 1973's price rise would run up against huge opposition from OPEC's more populous members (Iran, Nigeria, Venezuela), whose budgets could not stand the strain.

The danger with Russia is that it combines a dangerous level of military power with dependence on oil and could become so impoverished by the global energy transition that it lashes out, its rulers trying to placate/distract the country's suffering population. This would be a classic tale of losers. The collateral damage of climate change would thus be not direct (e.g. methane release from melting tundra) but indirect, catalysing military conflagration.

Too much, too late – the chief risk from climate change

The G7's response to the IEA's recent call for the world to follow a 'narrow path' to net-zero GHG emissions by 2050, thus (on the IEA's own analysis) limiting global warming to 1½° by then, was feeble for the reasons suggested above. But grounds for optimism lie in the evident seriousness of the Biden administration, together with the clear drift of business opinion and the courts in favour of taking seriously the threat of climate change. As regards business, the election of anti-denialist directors to the board of

Exxon is a clear rebuke by investors to the company that is the chief bastion of denialist business-as-usual activity and lobbying. This suggests that the current concern among investors about ESG-based investing (ESG – environmental, social and governance) is more than just window dressing or greenwashing – to use the current slur. On the legal front can be cited both a recent Dutch decision against Shell (an Anglo-Dutch company) and Germany's Federal Court of Justice finding that too much of the burden of fighting climate change was at the expense of future generations, and mandating that this be corrected.

Against this rosier view of prospective action must be set a number of points.

- The G7 limiting its commitment to ending fossil-fuel generating facilities to coal only, not fossil fuels generally, which would include 'transitional' gas-fuelled power plants.
- The G7 and associated countries committed to net zero by 2050 covering only a minority of emissions, so that this commitment would see global temperatures rise by 2.1°, quite a bit more than the 1½° desired limit by that date.
- China's commitment to net zero by 2060 ensuring the likely increase in the global temperature by 2050 will be above the IEA's target, which has also not been endorsed by other LDCs in the G20.
- The risk of destructive counter-action by OPEC or Russia. As the IEA makes clear, global compliance with its programme is needed for the net-zero goal to be reached.
- The need for worldwide adoption of carbon taxes to achieve net zero, especially bearing in mind that no new taxes (or

increased taxes) have been accepted in the US since the early 1990s, when George Bush Senior, a Republican president, pushed through a gasoline tax increase having been elected with a pledge of 'no new taxes – read my lips', causing his party to blame that tax increase for his 1992 election loss to Bill Clinton. It is not clear if the Republicans in the current US Senate have the votes to prevent any carbon tax by means of a filibuster, but as Biden has not picked up the carbon-tax baton, it is future Senate compositions that are relevant.

Given these obstacles to the goal of net zero by 2050, it is unlikely to be achieved. The current level of carbon in the earth's atmosphere, a little above 400 parts per million (ppm), is close to that prevailing a few million years ago in the Pliocene era, when for example plants were growing relatively close to the South Pole in a region where the average temperature is now −39°. If net zero is achieved some time after mid-century, the atmospheric carbon will be well above 400ppm, implying continued major global warming even if the fight against climate change is continued aggressively into an era of net negative stretching well into the twenty-second century. The time period for the full effects of GHGs to be felt is measured in millennia, not just centuries.

It is worth cataloguing the likely effects of varying degrees of global warming in order to assess at what point the world might collectively decide on drastic measures that will reasonably be described as too much, too late. The list below is culled from Mark Lynas' book *Six Degrees*, in which he discusses the likely effects of global warming according to its eventual scale: by 1°, 2°, 3°, etc. My list stops at 3°, as that takes the projection far enough into the future (probably the end of this century) and into dramatic enough damage to make it highly likely that drastic measures will be accepted and taken.

1° (a level already reached, with 1½° possible by 2025)

- South-west US desertification
- Gulf Stream slows or ceases (weakens this century, ends in the twenty-second century)
- Mountain glaciers melt (Kilimanjaro has lost 80 per cent over 100 years, cutting Kenyan water supply)
- Sahara extends, although cultivation may be helped by summer monsoons
- Arctic melts (with only a minor effect on global sea level as ice density is like water)
- Queensland rainforest loses species, also South Africa
- Hurricanes in the South Atlantic (unprecedented, unlike Katrina, etc. in the Caribbean and southern US)
- Disappearing islands

2°

- Gobi desert expands in China, northern China loses water
- Gasification of sea water, shellfish gradually wiped out
- Mediterranean becomes arid with forest fires (2003 European heatwave a taster for this, as may also prove true of 2021)
- Greenland ice melts by mid-twenty-second century, Miami, central London, much of Manhattan, Shanghai, Mumbai and Bangkok under water

- Struggle (war?) for the newly liquid Arctic
- Indian water crisis (aquifers dry up) as Himalayan snowmelt wanes, monsoons more violent
- Andean ice melt dries up in Peru, etc.
- Californian water supply dries up, although offset by increased food crops in north-central US
- General death of species, many because migration north is too slow

$3°$

- Huge desert in southern Africa and Amazon basin, fires widespread
- Northern India, Pakistan hit by loss of Himalayan snowmelt, Colorado snowmelt flow reduced
- Storms everywhere
- Rising sea level drowns New York region, London, Holland, Australian cities
- Runaway global warming starts – tipping point as carbon (methane) in soil released, waterlogged peat dies and emits, methane emissions from tundra
- Tropical diseases (much more dangerous than Covid-19) flourish

Appendix 1 gives a summary of Bill Gates' description of what needs to be done to get to net zero. As the list above makes clear, the achievement of net zero will need to be followed promptly by enunciation of a net-negative target to avoid the knock-on damage of the global warming that has already happened over the past quarter-millennium and is continuing to happen now. Most obviously because of the damage likely from land loss as the sea level rises both in coastal regions and in many cases further inland, but also for a myriad of other reasons (partially ecological, partly humanitarian), it will be important not just to get to net zero, as is clearly achievable with the right policies, but also to reverse much of the global warming that has already occurred. If policies to achieve net zero are kept in place to drive GHG emissions down below levels that are naturally absorbed by plants, then the worst long-term damage from climate change experienced by mid-century, both by humanity and the broader environment, can be avoided. It is a tall order, but feasible, necessary – and urgent.

Select bibliography to Essay 2

Gates, Bill, *How to Avoid a Climate Disaster*, Allen Lane, 2021
Goodhart, David, *Head, Hand, Heart*, Allen Lane, 2020
Jamieson, Dale, *Reason in a Dark Time*, Oxford University Press, 2014
Lovelock, James, *Novacene*, Allen Lane, 2019
Lynas, Mark, *Six Degrees*, Harper Perennial, 2007–8
Nelles, David & Serrer, Christian, *Small Gases, Big Effect*, Particular Books, 2021 (English), (orig. *Kleine Gase – Große Wirkung*, 2018)
Ord, Toby, *The Precipice*, Bloomsbury Publishing, 2020

Appendix 1

Bill Gates' 'to do' list

In this appendix the list of things needing to be done to get to zero carbon emissions is presented, based on Gates' analysis of the sources of man-made atmospheric GHG increases.

Industry (notably steel, cement and plastics)	31%
Electric power generation	27%
Agriculture (notably animal husbandry)	19%
Transport (surface and air)	16%
Premises: heating and cooling	7%

The 100 per cent that these percentages add up to is 51 billion tons a year of GHGs, and relates to 2019. The violent Covid-19 recession of 2020 may have lowered this a bit. Most of the man-made sources of emissions take the form of CO_2, which the *BP Statistical Review of World Energy* (henceforth the *BP Annual*) gives as just over 34 billion tons in 2019. Other GHGs include methane, more than eighty times as virulent as a GHG than CO_2 for the first twenty years, though also much less long lived in the atmosphere, and such gases as nitrous oxide (which can arise from over-application of fertilisers in growing 'green revolution' crops), which is 265 times more virulent than CO_2 as a GHG.

The breakdown of sources of GHGs differs between analyses. A very useful little summary of climate change by two Friedrichshafen Germans, David Nelles and Christian Serrer in *Small Gases, Big Effect*, gives the following analysis.

Industry	37%
Transport	23%
	(roads 17%, planes and ships 2½% each, other 1%)
Services	11%
Household	12%
Other	17%

This analysis applies to CO_2 emissions only. The book also breaks this down by fossil-fuel source – 44 per cent coal, 35 per cent oil and 21 per cent gas – and by country. This last breakdown is more controversial, since advanced economies have in effect exported much of their CO_2-producing activities to developing nations, but the authors helpfully provide a cumulative analysis based on CO_2 emissions in 1918–2012. Both are shown below.

	Current	Cumulative (1918–2012)
China	29%	12%
USA	14%	26%
EU (incl. UK)	10%	22%

India	7%	3%
Russia	5%	8%
Others	35%	29%

Based on the CO_2 table above, the chief point is the one made on page 74 that LDCs (and not just China) have a particular grievance vis-à-vis climate change, namely that they have contributed very little towards it, but are likely to suffer seriously from it.

The advantage of Bill Gates' book for economic analysis of what needs to be done is that he goes through the major sources of GHG emissions individually, and explains the steps needed to eliminate them, with a description for many of what he calls the 'green premium' – the percentage extra cost of the item made or performed with zero GHG emissions, versus current business as usual.

This appendix summarises Gates' material relevant to economic and political analysis. As the basic thrust of the zero-GHG goal is to use wherever possible electricity from renewables, primarily solar panels, wind power (onshore and offshore) and nuclear – hydropower is an important renewable source, but with only limited expansion potential – Gates inverts the two largest sources of GHGs, industry and electric power generation, to consider electricity first. This appendix will follow his order, but it must be remembered that his book's apparent purpose is to describe what is needed to restore business as usual, for the most part in America, but globally as well. While this is a perfectly legitimate goal and shows a refreshing reluctance to concede the argument to puritanism, there will be some aspects of BAU that are in direct conflict with the zero-GHG goal.

Electricity generation

In 2019 the energy sources of 99 per cent of the world's electricity, per the *BP Annual*, were: coal 36 per cent, natural gas 23 per cent, hydro 16 per cent, nuclear 10 per cent, oil 3 per cent and renewables (excluding hydro) 10 per cent. These shares add up to 98 per cent; rounding accounts for it not being 99 per cent.

Fossil fuels are subsidised in a variety of ways in various countries: for example, by 100 per cent first-year depreciation of drilling costs in the US (for tax purposes; normally, such capex would be depreciated over the life of the facilities), a concessionary value added tax rate on utilities in the UK, and so forth, perhaps the most spectacular examples being ultra-low oil and petrol prices for domestic users in many Middle Eastern oil states. Gates cites the IEA's estimate of $400 billion (about ½ per cent of gross world product/income) for global subsidies of fossil fuels in 2018. Coal-fired power stations are still being built, in China for example, where electricity is subsidised and coal consumption and output were up 2.8 times between 1999 and 2019; comparable gains in coal usage were seen in India, and in Indonesia the same twenty years saw coal consumption rise by more than eight times, from less than a third of India's in 1999 to 18 per cent more by 2019.

Yet, as the chart on page 2 shows, the wave of government financial support for wind power and solar-panel electricity has helped drop the all-up cost of solar-panel-derived electricity down below $60 per megawatt-hour (MWh) since 2019 – roughly the cost level for electricity based on coal and natural gas. Solar-panel electricity has shown the biggest decline in cost. It is now less than one sixth of what it was as recently as 2010. But onshore wind has come down by half, and remains marginally the cheaper of the two – when the wind is blowing!

That little aside, 'when the wind is blowing', introduces the large-scale technical problems to be solved if we are to take full advantage of the renewable-energy opportunities, of which zero-GHGs is not the only one, simply the most important. The natural time to turn lights on is when it gets dark, at which point the sun is not shining, so electricity is not being generated by solar panels. Of course, turning on the lights is not the only reason we need electricity at night-time – maybe not even the most important, as many industrial and business processes need electricity all night, though demand is indeed less in the wee hours.

The difficulties raised by intermittency of supply as between day and night can be solved, at considerable cost with current battery technology, and no doubt that extra cost can be cut by new techniques if the incentives are right. But the seasonal difference between the average hours of sunlight in summer and winter can be large in many advanced economies – Gates cites northerly parts of Canada and Russia where summer sunlight is about twelve times that of winter, versus Quito which has no such seasonality and his own Seattle home where the factor is two times. He also gives as an example that batteries to power Tokyo for three days could cost the same $400 billion (½ per cent of world product) that is the current full-year level of government subsidy for fossil fuels. And who is to say that a storm in Tokyo would only last three days?

How fast is electricity usage likely to grow? Leaving aside existing industrial and household uses, which are growing fast anyhow, the zero-GHG goal involves using electrical power for multiple new purposes, from steel making to transport. What else is going to drive all those vehicles we are being urged, maybe soon compelled, to buy? One answer could be hydrogen, if the huge technical problems of its zero-GHG production and its storage can be solved. (Hydrogen molecules can penetrate metals, so containing them at acceptable rates of loss is not easy.) But a reasonable thirty-year projection of 2050 electricity usage worldwide must put it up by four times. The twenty years of this century so far has seen it grow by 1.8 times, i.e. by 80 per cent (3 per cent a year, at which rate the thirty years to 2050 would see demand up nearly 2½ times). Zero GHG requires huge increases in the range of electricity application, in many cases to functions for which it is a lot less well suited than fossil-fuel energy or even its applications to date.

What is clear from any discussion of supply intermittency, as well as the geographical facts of sunlight hours, the spatial demands of solar farms, the sporadic nature of wind power and so forth, is that the key areas for innovation in renewable electricity lie in transmission and especially storage. Even within a continental country like the US, transmission will be an issue. If engineers can provide high-powered transmission facilities that will take power from solar farms in the south-west to colder regions like the Midwest and New England, states' rights will become an issue – as we have seen recently in Texas, which has insisted on its own, separate electricity system, which was knocked out for several days in February 2021 by fluke cold weather. As has been learned in many famines, it is distribution that fails, not basic availability of supply. In the Texan blackouts the state could not tap into power available elsewhere.

The prospect of major power lines across the US has broad environmental implications too. Putting them underground is massively costly, not least because power lines get hot, and in a confined space underground this can melt the metal. Bearing in mind that existing energy producers, from Exxon down to the smallest shale fracker, will be lobbying hard against zero-GHG measures, and that environmentalists have recently strongly opposed north–south pipelines in North America, it is not hard to see major political problems arising from the need to transmit electricity across the country.

In Europe and Japan techniques for transmission and storage of electricity will be crucial to the zero-GHG goal. Suppose the Saharan state of Chad (currently threatened by civil war) becomes the Saudi Arabia of solar power, its chief market will be in Europe. Solving the transmission and storage issues in that case may turn out to be a largely technical matter. But in any solution for comparable problems in Japan and South Korea, for example, ugly politics and troubled history are likely to rear their heads – though money will be an important solvent. For environmentalists, the zero-GHG possibility that is most controversial will always be nuclear electricity, which could in principle be zero GHG and also dodges the intermittency problems. But massive expansion of nuclear power generation is unlikely to be accepted, though increasingly dire consequences of global warming may change totally the terms of the debate on this (and everything else).

The use of electrolysis to generate hydrogen from water is one, much-mooted solution to the storage problem. Hydrogen being a key input to fuel-cell batteries, peak electricity could then be switched on, using the hydrogen during non-peak periods. But the energy derived arises as the hydrogen combines with oxygen to generate electricity (and water), and a process that uses electricity to turn water into hydrogen and then uses the gas to combine with oxygen to get electric power necessarily loses a lot of the original power along the way. For example, cars running on fuel cells from hydrogen are paying the equivalent of petrol/gasoline at $5.60 a gallon, 40 per cent more than the current Californian price, itself one of the highest in the US.

In spite of all these problems that need to be solved if zero GHG is to be achieved, the fact remains that the enormous recent progress in solar/wind technology may bring huge benefits to the global south, where there is plenty of sunshine and room for solar farms. In all regions of the world except Europe and the Pacific-rim countries, there is plenty of sunshine and room to take care of a large multiple of any possible future energy needs – at low cost now, likely to be even lower in future. This point includes the three big ones, China, USA and India. But economic potential from cheap solar power will rise most in Africa and Latin America. Unlike the grim consequences of Covid-19, the faster growth of poorer countries should continue the paradoxical pattern of 1999–2019 in which the world's distribution of income got more equal, even though inequality increased in most individual countries.

Carbon capture and storage

Carbon capture from a particular point or process is an existing technology, but expensive and less than totally effective: generally, only about 90 per cent of the GHGs are captured and stored. But this technology may be made economic if a carbon tax is levied, in cases where the green premium is high, as with cement manufacture (see page 119). Carbon capture will always be needed for some purposes in a zero-GHG world, and it will always be an added expense. Clearly, technological improvement can lower the cost, as could the simple fact of people focusing on it, and doing it in much greater volume than hitherto. But the technological improvement will be faster and greater if the incentives are right. This could either mean the benefit of avoiding a carbon tax, or public-sector subsidy. In principle, a private-sector solution arising in the carbon-tax scenario is likely to be superior.

An alternative technique is direct air capture (DAC), in which air is blown over material that absorbs CO_2, which is then stored. In principle, this is less efficient than carbon capture, as the latter operates at the point where carbon, or CO_2, is concentrated, while the density of CO_2 in the atmosphere is inherently less. The cost of DAC is at least $200 per ton, so as of now it puts the cost of decarbonising the world's annual emissions (some 50 billion tons) at $10 trillion, one eighth of world GDP – not a bad bargain, it could be argued, considering the risks from global warming and climate change. But Gates thinks it is realistic that this cost can be cut to $100/ton.

Industry, notably steel, cement and plastics

Industrial processes are the largest source of GHGs in the world. Steel, for example, is made by melting iron ore and coke at 1,700 degrees Celsius; the coke then releases its carbon which bonds with the iron to make steel. The iron ore has released its oxygen, and that combines with the 'spare' carbon to become CO_2. With current processes, each ton of steel involves 1.8 tons of CO_2 emissions. The world's steel output of 1.9 billion tons in 2019 could rise to 2.8 billion in 2050, with five billion tons of CO_2 emissions in a BAU scenario. In 2019, CO_2 emissions from steel manufacture were about 10 per cent of the total world's CO_2 emissions of 34 billion tons – in China, making more than half the world's steel, the ratio is more like 18 per cent.

Cement is the key product in producing concrete – with added gravel, sand and water. Cement is made by heating limestone to about 1,500 degrees Celsius, so that the calcium in the limestone forms calcium oxide, the other main product of this process being CO_2. Here again Chinese infrastructure demand puts it in first place, with 2.2 billion tons of cement out of the world's 4.1 billion, with India's 320 million tons in second place. Every ton of cement means a ton of CO_2 emissions, so cement, ineluctably involving CO_2 emissions, was a larger source of CO_2 emissions in 2019 than steel manufacture.

China's CO_2 emissions from making cement are estimated by my TS Lombard colleagues to be 16 per cent of its total, a little below the 18 per cent ratio for steel, but above the global 12 per cent ratio of 4.1 billion tons of CO_2 emissions to the 34 billion world total. With China's economy shifting in emphasis from metal bashing to services and tech (and from capex to consumer spending, on the demand side) its construction boom may fall back somewhat from now on. But the rest of the EMs could pick up the slack, so CO_2 emissions from cement making could remain at the current rate of about 4 billion tons indefinitely.

The pollution problem with plastics arises partly from the feature that reduces their climate-change contribution. Around half the carbon involved in making them is compounded into the plastic, where it is combined with hydrogen and oxygen. This makes it very durable, taking centuries to break down, meanwhile polluting the oceans and landfill disposal sites. But that means its green premium vis-à-vis climate change is less than for steel and cement.

'Clean' (i.e. green) electricity only goes a little of the way to replacing fossil fuels in steel and cement manufacturing plants; the bulk of the CO_2 emissions arise because of the extreme heat required – electricity cannot do this with current technology – and the role of CO_2 emissions as a manufacturing by-product. So carbon capture techniques will be needed to get to zero GHG. The price and green premium information from Gates' book is (for a ton of each material):

	Price	*CO_2 emissions ratio*	*Green premium*	*Percentage green price*
Ethylene plastic	$1,000	1.3	9–15	$1,087–$1,155
Steel	$750	1.8	16–29	$871–$964
Cement	$125	1.0	75–140	$219–$300

Similar calculations will have to be made for makers of glass, paper, aluminium, etc. The key point is that zero GHG will almost certainly require prolonged carbon capture, at least for cement, so that will be an area requiring intense technical innovation over the next thirty years, well beyond that needed to make renewables electricity universally available and to make all processes use electric power where possible.

Farming and forestry

With the world population now 7.8 billion people, and forecast to rise to 11 billion by 2100, though by then it should have stopped growing, the GHG emissions from farming come into focus as a potential source of conflict between zero GHG and feeding people. Paul Ehrlich's 1968 book *The Population Bomb*, which forecast mass starvation, had already been invalidated by the green revolution in agriculture, for which Norman Borlaug won the Nobel Peace Prize in 1970. The yields from introducing the new crops soared in the second half of the 1960s and disproved Ehrlich's Malthusian thesis. But climate change could revive such neo-Malthusian views, not least because of the risks of desertification it entails.

A near-40 per cent rise in world population over the balance of this century will require more than a 40 per cent rise in food output. As poorer people in EMs gain higher incomes, they upgrade their diets – not least by eating more meat, which means rearing more animals, invariably consuming more calories in their food intake than humans get by eating the resulting meat. Yet animal husbandry is a potent source of GHGs – and not just CO_2, as the chief GHG in a cow's belch or fart is methane. With a billion cattle round the world, just this GHG emission is equivalent in global-warming effect to 2 billion tons of CO_2 – not far short of steel making's effects. The kind of breakdown of plant cellulose done by cows' multiple stomachs is shared with other grazing animals, notably sheep. But over and beyond that lies the GHG emissions in animal excrement, nitrous oxide most of all, but also methane, sulphur and ammonia (hence its use as fertiliser in the pre-fertiliser era).

There are self-correcting aspects in all this, just as there were in the nineteenth-century invalidation of Malthus. (With whom Adam Smith and David Ricardo – and not just Karl Marx – agreed about the probable 'immiseration of the masses', it should be noted. Who says economists, even great ones, cannot be collectively wrong?) The simple fact was that getting better off cut the attraction of large families. Now it seems cattle in South America emit up to five times more GHGs than in North America (or Europe, it should be noted especially by people quite reasonably hostile to US livestock farming and abbatoir practices). The US breeds are better, and the feed is better. So people getting better off remains a good thing, as in the nineteenth century, even for Argentine steaks – but that will certainly not be enough by itself.

Apart from meat eating, an emotional subject for vegetarians, who have not been slow to use climate-change dangers to promote their cause, the green revolution has turned out to be anti-green (in the modern sense of green) in promoting huge, often wasteful, use of artificial fertilisers. The manufacture of ammonia (NH_3) should get cheaper as a result of green electricity's potentially lower cost, but it is estimated that less than half the fertiliser used in agriculture is actually absorbed by plants, stimulating their growth. The rest gets into water, with resulting pollution, or into the atmosphere in the form of nitrous oxide (N_2O_3 – laughing gas), a GHG that is 265 times more effective as a global warming agent than CO_2.

While scientists are working on green substitutes for fertilisers, the nitrogen element is likely to remain in all of them, so this wastage effect on climate change is likely to remain. (Precisely targeted fertiliser use may gradually help a little, but LDC farmers may take a long time to change their habits.) This brings the issue back to population growth as a stimulant to global warming. Obviously, food demand and production is closely related to population trends, but so is another major cause of climate change: deforestation, much of which, whether in Brazil's Amazon basin, Nigeria or Indonesia, amounts to land clearance for food crops. The Brazilian case is well publicised, the Amazon basin being the world's largest rainforest, and the clearances (often by fire, which adds directly to atmospheric GHGs) are done for a variety of farming reasons, including more recently the illegal production of soya for export to China, where it is fed to the burgeoning pig population, the pigs being value-added soya, and inclined to belch like most livestock.

Transport

The IEA report says that the 1.5° target for total global warming by 2050 requires 20 per cent of cars on the world's roads to be electric by 2030. Given the conspicuous role of cars in everyday life and the attention paid as a result to their climate-change impact, this is one target that is clearly achievable. In fact, in many countries it is being legislated for. Nor need consumers suffer significant loss of real income as a result, given the likely further fall in solar-based electricity in future years.

About three quarters of the transport contribution to climate change (given as 16 per cent of the total by Gates, but 23 per cent by Nelles and Serrer) is from road transport, and a little over one tenth each is attributable to planes and ships, with a small contribution from trains. The snag with the electric solution is that it is unlikely to work for trucks without a large rise in transport costs. For example, Gates cites a study suggesting that an electric truck doing a 600-mile journey on a single charge would have to take one quarter less cargo, and 900 miles could not be done, owing to the huge weight of batteries needed. Gates rightly makes much of the sheer efficiency and cheapness of liquid fossil fuels. With current technology and use of advanced biofuels the green premium vis-à-vis diesel is 100 per cent, so the fuel cost of truck transport would double.

When it comes to planes, advanced biofuels' green premium vis-à-vis current jet fuel prices is 140 per cent, so the fuel cost of flying would be nearly 2½ times today's. A battery-powered airliner is a pipe dream, as at best it would be much slower and more limited in range than current airliners (which can carry 300 passengers at 600-plus mph for close on 20 hours on one tank of jet fuel): the batteries needed would weigh 35 times more than the jet fuel, a ratio that might come down with better battery technology, but not enough to ensure lift-off for electric airliners, though smaller battery-driven planes are feasible. Given the penalty to air travel already arising in the aftermath of Covid-19, this kind of statistic should reinforce the surge of video conferencing at the expense of business travel, which pays a disproportionate share of the revenues of airlines and hotels. If the fuel cost is supplemented by a carbon tax, as this book suggests, the era of mass, cheap travel may be behind us. Aircraft manufacturers are engaged heavily in research into advanced biofuels and hydrogen, and hydrogen-driven airliners are possible by 2050.

The one tenth of transport-related GHG emissions arising from shipping is different again. International shipping is cheap and dirty – largely unregulated, as ships use flags of convenience from the likes of Panama, and are driven by bunker fuel which is what's left over when all the higher-value products of petroleum have been extracted. This is the equivalent of Germany's recent reliance on sulphur-laden lignite – brown coal – as a result of emotional hostility to existing nuclear generating plants after Japan's Fukushima disaster in 2011. But containerised shipping transport is very cheap as a result. Steps to clean it up will raise the cost of world trade, cutting its volume or at least its growth and thus global welfare.

Home heating and cooling

Heating homes (and offices and other work premises) in winter and the year-round provision of hot water is an offshoot of the points already made. In Europe, the primary fuel now is natural gas. In future, electricity will probably predominate, in many cases in the form of heat pumps (the reverse of a fridge). If 'clean' gas or liquid fuels – e.g. hydrogen-based – can be developed to heat homes and other premises, that may prove to be the low-cost route away from fossil fuels. Otherwise a solution to the intermittency problem has to be found and applied, either cheaper electricity storage or transmission, as solar electricity in winter (as well as at night) will be in short supply in northern climes. The migration of much of the American retired population to hotter parts of the country could in effect shift the demand to the supply in this respect.

In Japan and America, 90 per cent of homes have air conditioners, and in Korea the ratio is nearly as high, well over 80 per cent. These are heavy users of electricity, and the demand for them can only go up as developing economies get better off, and the world hotter. But there is what Gates calls a 'negative green premium' in this, as green electricity gets cheaper than fossil-fuelled power generation. For the 7 per cent of GHG emissions that emanate from homes and buildings, excluding their original construction, the main shift needed will be towards more electricity, with development of green fuels probably secondary.

Appendix 2

Carbon taxes and inequality

In taxation, as with most government policies, there is what should happen and there is what will happen. It is safe to say that without some financial penalty for emission of GHGs, net zero will never happen. A carbon tax is simply the clearest way to motivate achievement of net zero by introducing such a penalty. Unlike cap and trade systems to put a price on carbon emissions, it offers a greater degree of certainty to businesses and households making the key decisions, as well as the other advantages mentioned (page 95). So, taking the pledges to achieve net zero as being both sincere and likely to be achieved – if only too late, via policies that are too much, too late (see page 103) – it is best to start by outlining the optimal carbon-tax proposal, and then seeing what might actually happen.

The optimal carbon-tax policy package would:

- Be inevitably regressive, i.e. hitting the poor more than the rich.
- Offset assistance to poorer people through wealth taxation, always a better economic incentive than taxes on the income

from wealth, as it severely discourages unproductive asset usage.
- Offset carbon-tax revenues by reducing other taxes – e.g. abolishing taxes on corporate profits, so getting rid of one of the major routes to tax avoidance by internationally operating firms, a measure that would require a higher rate of the wealth tax mentioned in the previous point.

Why is this not likely to happen? For several reasons, the first of which is that wealth taxes are always strongly resisted (and avoided) as being the 'thin edge of the wedge' by which the majority in a democracy can make short-term gains at the expense of a wealthy but highly productive minority. (Even refining a wealth tax down to a land tax – land after all cannot be relocated to the Cayman Islands – leaves unaffected the thin-end-of-the-wedge point.)

Apart from the fundamental opposition to wealth taxes, any tax policy programme to get to net zero must be politically feasible in the US to be credible. Resistance there to taxes is strong; it will take a massive political shift even to get an effective carbon tax implemented, let alone a tax on wealth as well. And it is worth noting that the US is more dependent on corporate income taxes than most advanced economies. Arguably, they are used as a stealthy form of indirect taxation largely reflected in prices and pre-tax profits and therefore fall on consumers in a similar fashion to value added (or sales) taxes elsewhere, precisely because of the US resistance to raising any taxes at all from actual people.

Resistance to net-zero GHGs in the US will be both

encouraged and discouraged by the combination of market forces and the administrative complications of carbon taxes – of cap and trade schemes too, for that matter. Not only will carbon taxes require approval by both houses of Congress – itself a tall order – but the proper identification of the carbon content of imports, on which the carbon tax will have to be levied (as is already proposed by the EU) will also enable opponents of the tax to say it breaches the World Trade Organisation's rules. This should give opponents of net zero plenty of scope for obstruction, and it could turn the too much, too late scenario for dealing with climate change (page 103) into the mainstream view of how events will materialise in practice.

Contrariwise, discouraging net-zero resistance will be the obsolescence of much fossil-fuel activity, now that renewables electricity is cheaper. In the US more than other advanced economies, established businesses can readily and quickly be ousted by newcomers. And much of the US energy infrastructure is old and outdated, suggesting the cost of its write-off and replacement will be less than in many countries.

In the absence of a carbon tax, any attempt at net-zero GHG emissions by 2050 in the US will mean gale-force federal spending on research into such items as carbon storage, whether by direct spending or the incentive of tax breaks (so-called tax expenditure). The millions of promised jobs will not just grow on trees. So simple fiscal considerations may encourage the federal authorities to pursue a carbon tax. With current annual emissions of five billion tons, a tax rate of the potential $75–$100/ton rate would generate revenue of some $375–500 billion, an impressive 1¾–2½ per cent of the $20 trillion GDP. For comparison, the corporate income tax yield is a little over half this, about 1.1 per cent of GDP. And tax levied on the carbon content of imports will add to the revenue gains. Obviously, if the net-zero target is achieved, the yield of the carbon tax will dwindle to zero too, so permanent diminution of the tax base could be unwise. But meanwhile economic activity and federal revenues will gain from replacement of obsolescent stranded assets.

Index

Page references in *italics* indicate graphs.
GFC indicates global financial crisis (2007–09).
GHG indicates greenhouse gases.

Africa 21, 50, 67, 71, 75, 76, 84–5, 106, 107, 116. *See also individual nation name*
ageing, population 60–4
agriculture, GHG emissions and 7, 10, 93, 95, 109, 110, 120–2
AI (artificial intelligence) 31, 86
air travel 40, 98, 123–4
ammonia (NH_3) 121–2
Antarctica 8
Arctic 8, 95, 106, 107
Asian financial crisis (1997) 44
'Asian Tiger' economies 13, 25. *See also individual nation name*
Australia 12, 25, 26, 107
automatic stabilisers 14

Baker, James 28

Balkans 28
battery technology 1, 45, 46, 113, 116, 123–4
Bentham, Jeremy 89–90
Biden, Joe 20, 25, 28, 45–6, 53, 97, 100–01, 103, 105
biofuels 123, 124
blame, climate change and 7
Blinken, Antony 28
bond market 43, 45, 51
Borlaug, Norman 120
BP Statistical Review of World Energy 109, 112
Brazil 8, 122
budget deficits
 China and 16–17, *17*, 22, 24, 32, 56, 63
 Covid-19 and 22, 24, 32, 43, 47, *48*, 49, 50, 51–4, *52*, 56, 57, 63, 64–5
 demand/growth, reliance on to generate 4–5, *4*, *5*, 13, 22, 47, *48*, 49–50
 EA nations and 14–15, 22, 47, *48*, 58

GFC and 4–5, 12, 13, 14–15,
  19, 63
growth, slowing of linked to
  56–8
inflation and 43, 51, 52–4
Japan and *5*, 13, *14*, 17, 56–8,
  63, 64–5
savings and 13, 50, 57, 61, 63, 64
US and 13, 15, 18–19, 22, 47–9,
  48, 51–4, *52*, 58
business travel 35, 37–40, *38*, 55,
  59, 124

'cake-ism' 26–7
capital spending (capex) 3, 4, 5,
  15, 16, 19, *29*, 30, 49, 53, 57, 65,
  112, 118–19
carbon dioxide (CO_2) emissions
  accounting 69, 97, 98
  cap and trade systems 93, 94–7,
    126, 128
  capture and storage 97, 117
  net-zero targets *see* net-zero
    carbon emissions
  rate of 66–7
  sources of man-made
    atmospheric 109–25
  taxes/price *see* carbon taxes
carbon taxes 63
  carbon capture and storage
    and 117
  fiscal deflation and 62
  inequality and 126–9
  motivating decarbonisation
    and 69, 92–9, 104–5
  transport and 124
  UK, as opportunity for 99–101

cement manufacturing 7, 96, 109,
  117, 118–20
China 8, 9, 122
  Australia, bullying of 26
  carbon dioxide (CO_2)
    emissions, rate of 6, 46,
    66–7, 74, 75, 94, 96, 97, 99,
    110, 111, 112, 118–19
  cement manufacture 96, 118–19
  coal-fired power stations 46, 112
  consumer spending 24, 30–1,
    32, 34, 119
  Covid-19, economy, post- 34,
    41, 46, 47, 56, 58, 59
  Covid-19 recession (2020) and
    12, 21–32, *24*, *29*
  de-Americanisation 32
  debt levels/budget deficits *17*,
    22, 24, 32, 56, 63
  'dual-circulation' policy 24, *24*,
    30, 59
  EU–China Comprehensive
    Agreement on Investment 25
  European economies reliance
    on 23, 25, 26, 28–9, 32
  GDP growth 15–17, *16*, 22, 23,
    24, 31, 47, 56
  GDP, shares of *29*
  GFC and 12–13, 15–18, *16*, *17*
  Hong Kong and 25–6
  human rights policies 25–6
  import ratio 29–30, *29*
  import substitution 28, 30,
    32–3
  inflation and *41*, 44
  nationalism and climate change
    in 102

net-zero carbon emissions
target 6, 46, 94, 104
population growth 75
Regional Comprehensive
Economic Partnership
(RCEP) 25, 27
renewable energy sector 20–1,
75, 116
steel manufacture 96, 97, 99,
118
tech sector 30, 31–2, 47, 59, 118
2° warming in 106
US, trade war with (2018–) 9,
10, 12, 19, 20–1, 24–5, *24*,
26–7, 28, 29, 33, 58–9, 68
wolf diplomacy 25–6
city centres 39, 55, 59
Clean Air Act (1956) 92, 98
climate change 66–129
carbon emissions *see* carbon
dioxide emissions
carbon taxes and *see* carbon
taxes
global warming, likely effects of
varying degrees of 105–8
How to Avoid a Climate Disaster
(Gates) and strategies to
mitigate 68–9, 72, 76, 84, 92,
93–4, 107, 109–25
LDC argument against
combatting 102–3
nationalism and 102–3
population growth and 87–92
speed of 71–2
Stern Report (2006) on 6,
68–9, 72–4, 82, 85
Clinton, Bill 105

Clinton, Hillary 18, 20
commodities
'commodity countries' 12, 16,
23
prices 13, 15, 23, 44–5, *45*
supercycle 13, 15, 44–5, *45*
Commodity Research Bureau
industrials sub-index 45
constructive ambiguity 25
consumer spending 22, 23, 24,
30–1, 32, 33–5, 40–2, 119
coral reefs 79
corporation tax 100, 101
Covid-19 5, 6, 10, 12, 20, 21
recession (2020) 12, 21–32, *24*,
29, 34, 56, 59
world economy, post-Covid
33–65
budget deficits and 5, 43, 47,
48, 49, 50, 51–4, *52*, 56, 57,
63, 64–5
business travel and *38*, 39–41
employment and 54–8
fragmentation of world
economy and 33, 47, 58–9
growth decline and
opportunities in 46–51, *48*
inflation and 40–6, *41*, *43*,
45, 51–4, *52*
population ageing and 60–2
return to normal 34–5
short-term policy 62–5, *64*
tech activity surge and 46–7,
59
working from home (WFH)
and 34–40, *36*, *38*, *39*, 54–5

debt
  budget deficits *see* budget
    deficits
  Covid-19 and 22, 24, 32, 35, 47,
    49, 53, 56–8, 63, 64–5
  GFC and 4–5, 5, 13–17, *14*, *17*
  non-financial debt as
    percentage of GDP, advanced
    economies 5
  savings and 13, 50, 57, 61, 63,
    64
deflation 4, 18, 60, 62
deforestation 122
de Gaulle, General 26
demand
  budget deficits and 1–5, 13, 22,
    27–8, 49
  Covid-19 and 33, 49–50, 53–4,
    59
  inflation and 53–4, 62
  renewable energy and 50–1
Democratic Party, US 18, 20,
  53
determinism, fallacy of 89, 90
devaluation 18, 27–8
direct air capture (DAC) 117
discount rate, future welfare 80,
  82–3, 87–8

EA (European Area)
  Covid-19 recession and 22, 23,
    25, *48*, 58, *64*
  GFC and 14–15, *14*
  See also European Union (EU)
Ehrlich, Paul: *The Population
  Bomb* 120
Einstein, Albert 90

electricity generation 69, 80, 94,
  121–2, 124–5
  fossil-fuelled 5, 67, 80, 94
  GHG emissions and 109, 111,
    112–16, 124–5
  renewable energy derived costs
    1, 2, *3*, 5–6, 11, 21, 45–7, 50–1,
    67, 68, 71, 75, 91, 119, 120,
    128
electrification
  developing countries and 50–1,
    64
  vehicles 46, 93, 98–9, 114, 122–4
emerging markets (EMs) 9, 21,
  23, *41*, 47, 58, 71, 74, 85, 96,
  119, 120
ESG (environmental, social and
  governance)-based investing
  104
euro crisis 14–15, 64
European Central Bank (ECB)
  27–8
European Parliament 25, 28
European Union (EU)
  carbon emission sources in 110
  carbon taxes in 94–5, 96, 97,
    101, 128
  China and 23, 25, 26, 28–9, 32
  Covid-19 recession and 23, 25,
    26, 28–9, 32, 34, 47
  debt/budget deficits in 13, 27–8,
    47, *48*, 63, 64
  demand weakness in 27–8, 47
  devaluation in 18, 27–8
  EU–China Comprehensive
    Agreement on Investment
    and 25

euro crisis 14–15, 64
export dependence in 28, 32, 47
GFC and 16
military spending in/defence of 27–8
renewable energy market 115, 116
Russia and 27
US and 26, 27–9
externalities 69, 70–1, 92
extinction, humanity 76, 79, 83, 85–6
Exxon 104, 115

fertiliser 110, 121–2
fiscal stimulus 18, 22, 47, 51
fragmentation, globalisation and 20–1, 28, 33, 47, 58, 59, 68
France *14*, 23, 25, 26, 58
Friedman, Milton 9

Gaia thesis 76, 85
gas, natural 1, *2*, 27, 45–6, 50, 69, 78, 92, 93, 94, 99, 104, 110, 112, 113, 116, 124–5
Gates, Bill:
How to Avoid a Climate Disaster 68–9, 72, 76, 84, 93, 94, 107, 109–25 'to do' list 109–25
Germany
budget deficits, constitutional amendment banning (2009) 14–15, 56
carbon taxes and 101
climate change, emergency programme to combat 28
Covid-19 and 23, 25, 27, 28–9, 32, 56
EU–China Comprehensive Agreement on Investment and 25
GFC and 12, 13, *14*, 15
Russia/Nord Stream 2 gas-pipeline project and 27
global financial crisis (GFC) (2007–09) 4–5, 12, 13, 15, 16–17, 19, 30, 44, 54, 57, 61, 63
globalisation 9, 10, 13, 19
fragmentation of 20–1, 28, 33, 47, 58, 59, 68
global warming 6–7, 8, 70, 71, 72, 74, 77, 78, 79, 80, 81, 82, 94, 103, 116, 117, 121, 122
likely effects of varying degrees of 105–8
Goldman Sachs 35
gold standard 58, 89
Granville, Christopher 26
greenhouse gas (GHG) emissions
net-zero *see* net-zero carbon emissions
sources of 7, 10, 93, 95, 109–25
See also carbon dioxide emissions *and individual nation name*
Greenland 8, 106
green revolution 10, 110, 120, 121
G7 47, 66, 94, 104
G20 66, 104

Heisenberg, Werner 89
Hong Kong 25–6
household energy usage 98

House of Representatives, US
  13, 14
housing market 37, 55
hydrogen 98, 114, 116, 119, 124,
  125

imports
  import ratio 30
  import substitution 28, 32
India 9, 34, 58, 66–7, 74, 75, 96,
  102, 107, 111, 112, 116
Indonesia 8, 112, 122
industrial processes 118–20
inequality 9–10, *10*, 23, 84–5, 116
  carbon taxes and 126–9
  indicators of reduced world *10*
  K-shaped effect and 54
inflation 4, 10, 19, 25, 33, 35,
  40–4, *41*, *43*, 45, *45*, 51–4, *52*,
  60, 62
  disinflation 4
  long-term threat of 51–4, *52*
  US forecast for 43–4, *43*
Intergovernmental Panel on
  Climate Change (IPCC) 8, 76,
  77, 82, 94
interest rates 4, 5, 35, 47, 49, 50,
  53, 56
International Energy Agency
  (IEA) 8, 72, 77–8, 94, 103–4,
  112, 122–3
Iran 44, 103

Japan 13, 17, 26–7
  budget deficits/debt 5, 13, *14*,
    17, 49, 56–7, 63, 64–5
  'cake-ism' and 26
  Chinese 'dual circulation'
    policy and 30, 32
  Covid-19 and *48*, 49, 56–7
  electricity use in 125
  GFC and 13, *14*
  import ratio 30
  nuclear generating plants 124
  population decline 61
  renewable energy and 75, 115
  savings in 57, 61, 63, 64
JP Morgan 35, 36, 39

Kerry, John 97
Keynes, John Maynard 3, 4, 10,
  18, 19, 43
Korea 23, 25, 26–7, 32, 71, 115, 125
K-shaped effect 54

less-developed countries (LDCs)
  7–8, 11, 73, 75, 76, 79, 80, 102,
  104, 111, 122
life expectancy 60
liquidity 41, 42, 50, 57
Lovelock, James 76: *Novacene*
  85, 86
Lynas, Mark: *Six Degrees* 77,
  105–7

Malthus, Thomas 7, 120, 121
Marx, Karl 3, 49, 51, 121
meat eating 120–2
Merkel, Angela 27
methane 7, 93, 95, 103, 107, 109,
  121
Microsoft Windows 97
monetarism 9, 10, 18–19, 43, 51, 54

nationalism 21, 24–5, 34, 46, 59
  combating climate change and
    102–3
neoliberalism 9. *See also*
  monetarism
net-negative carbon emissions 9,
  79, 82, 105, 107
net-zero carbon emissions 79, 82
  carbon taxes and 92, 93, 94,
    95, 96, 97, 98, 103, 104, 105,
    107–8, 126–9
  How to Avoid a Climate Disaster
    (Gates) and 68–9
  IEA report on net-zero
    greenhouse gases (GHGs) by
    2050/'narrow path' leading to
    8–9, 77, 103
  net-negative carbon emissions
    and 9, 79, 82, 105, 107
  stranded assets replacement
    and 5–6
Newtonian mechanics 90
Nordhaus, William 85
Nord Stream 2 gas-pipeline
  project 27

Obama, Barack 13, 18, 21, 53
OECD *4*, 15, *48*, 49, *64*
oil
  Big Oil 92
  crisis (1973–5) 19, 44, 103
  price 13, 19, 45, 46, 78, 103,
    104
online shopping 39, 55, 59
OPEC 78, 103, 104
Ord, Toby: *The Precipice* 85–6

Paris Agreement (2016) 46
pensions 61, 98
People's Bank of China 22
Philadelphia Federal Reserve 19
Pliocene era 105
Poincaré, Henri 90
population
  ageing 60–4
  growth 6–7, 9, 75–6, 82–3,
    87–92, 120–2
  shrinkage 74, 75–6, 81, 87
populism 10–11
poverty 9–10, *10*, 11, 61, 80
price gouging 41–2
productivity 1, 46–7, 55, 58, 59,
  64, 88
protectionism 20
Putin, Vladimir 27

Ramsey, Frank 3, 49, 82, 83, 86–7,
  89
Reading, Brian 85
recession 10, 12, 15, 33, 47, 54, 56,
  63, 67, 78, 109
  Covid-19 (2020) 21–32, *24*, *29*
Regional Comprehensive
  Economic Partnership (RCEP)
  25, 27
renewable energy
  carbon taxes and 93
  China and 20–1, 75, 116
  developing countries/global
    south, benefits to 50–1, 67,
    71, 75, 115, 116
  electricity generating costs from
    1, 2, 3, 5–6, 11, 45–6, 50–1,
    67, 68, 71, 75, 112–13, 123, 128

solar power 1, 2, 21, 45–6, 50, 67, 71, 75, 111, 112–13, 114–15, 116, 123, 125
wind power 1, 2, 45–6, 50, 67, 71, 75, 111, 112–13, 114, 116
Republican Party, US 13–14, 18, 64, 105
retirement 46, 60, 61, 125
Rogoff/Reinhart effect 49, 56, 57
Russia 8, 27, 78, 88, 102, 103, 104, 111, 113

Sanders, Bernie 20
Saudi Arabia 78, 102–3, 115
savings 3, 22, 49–50, 61–2
'savings glut' 13, 57, 63, 82
scientific fact 90
sea level 8–9, 70, 77, 80, 81, 95, 107, 108
Senate, US 13, 14, 105
Shanghai Composite 17
Shell 104
shipping 124
Sino–US trade war (2018–) 9, 10, 12, 19, 20–1, 24–5, *24*, 26–7, 28, 29, 33, 58–9, 68
Small Gases, Big Effect (David Nelles and Christian Serrer) 110
solar power 1, 2, 21, 45–6, 50, 67, 71, 75, 111, 112–13, 114–15, 116, 123, 125
South America 37, 50, 71, 121. *See also individual nation name*
steel manufacturing 7, 96, 97, 99, 109, 114, 118–20, 121
Stern Report (2006) 6, 68–9, 72–4, 82, 85

stranded assets 5–6, 46, 55, 71, 129
structural budget balances *14*, 15, 18, *48*, 63
subsidies 11, 62–3, 69, 70, 95, 112, 114, 117

Taiwan 23, 25–7, 32, 71
taxation 15, 52, 62
  carbon *see* carbon taxes
  corporation tax 100, 101
  Japanese consumption tax increase (2014) 61, 63
  tax neutrality 99
  Trump tax cuts 18–19
Tea Party, US 14, 18, 64
tech sector 1, 3, 10, 20, 23
  China and 30, 31–2, 47, 59, 118
  Covid-19 and 46–7, 59
time-value of money 82–3, 85–7, 90
Tobacco, Big 92
Trans-Pacific Partnership 25
Trump, Donald 18, 19, 20, 21, 24–5, 27, 28, 64
TS Lombard 2, *4*, *5*, *10*, *16*, 35–6, *36*, *38*, *39*, *41*, 42, *43*, 45, *48*, 51–2, *52*, 56, *64*, 118

Uighers 25–6
UK
  carbon taxes as opportunity for 99–101
  Covid-19, economy post- *48*, 58, 63, 64, *64*
  Covid-19 recession and 23
  GFC and 13, *14*, 63

VAT rate on energy utilities 98, 112
Ukraine 27
uncertainty principle 89
US
  agriculture in 121
  budget deficits in 1, 4–5, *5*, 13–15, *14*, 18, 47, *48*, 49, 51, 53–4
  carbon taxes and 101, 105, 127–8
  China, trade war with (2018–) 9, 10, 12, 19, 20–1, 24–5, *24*, 26–7, 28, 29, 33, 58–9, 68
  Covid-19 recession and 22, 23–5, 27–8
  Covid-19, world economy post- and 33, 34, 39–40, *39*, 42–9, *43*, *45*, *48*, 51–4, *52*, 56, 58–9, 64, 68
  economic forecast (May 2021) 42–3, *43*
  EU and 27–8
  Families Plan and Jobs Plan 53
  GDP growth, pre-Covid *48*
  GFC and 13, 15, 18, 19, 63
  global warming and 106, 107
  import ratio 30
  inflation and 42–5, *43*, *45*, 51–3
  infrastructure capex programmes in 53
  managed capitalism in 47
  mid-term elections (2010) 13, 53
  mid-term elections (2022) 53
  net-zero GHGs in, resistance to 127–8
  Paris accord on climate change and 46
  Presidential Election (2016) 18, 20
  Presidential Election (2020) 25
  renewable energy in 114–15, 116
  tech sector 31, 46–7, 59
  Trump tax cuts (2017) 18–19

VAT rate, energy utilities and 98, 112
Volcker, Paul 19, 44

weather events, extreme 6, 71, 91
welfare offset 62
wind power 1, 2, 45–6, 50, 67, 71, 75, 111, 112–13, 114, 116
working from home (WFH) 34–40, *36*, *38*, *39*, 54–5
World Bank 6, 9, *10*
World Trade Organisation (WTO) 97, 128

Yom Kippur War (1973) 44
yuan 18